Clarence H. Juergens

Bistro Style Cookery

Bistro Style Cookery

Michael Raffael

Northwood Publications Limited
London EC1V 7QA

Published 1978

© Northwood Publications Ltd and
Michael Raffael, 1978

ISBN 7198 2634 9

Menu illustrations by Dick Barnard

A 'Catering Times' Book

Printed and bound in Great Britain
by Eyre & Spottiswoode Ltd
Grosvenor Press, Cosham, Portsmouth.

Contents

Foreword

This collection of unusual recipes will, I hope, go a long way towards filling a noticeable gap in catering literature. Compiled by Michael Raffael, a regular contributor to *Catering Times*, the book is aimed at those restaurateurs who are endeavouring to fulfil that most difficult of culinary objectives – to offer an interesting or unusual dish at a modest price.

The recipes will be particularly suited to those who are operating bistro or bistro-style restaurants where the food served has to be simple, inexpensive but of a high quality. In compiling this book, Michael Raffael has taken account of the major problem facing the operator of this type of restaurant – the difficulty of finding skilled staff who can easily prepare high quality, inexpensive dishes.

The directions to each recipe, therefore, suggest the degree of time and skill needed to prepare the dish and give a comparative notion of the cost involved. All of the dishes have been tested. Not all of them may be suited to every restaurant, but the secret of a good chef/patron lies in his ability to take a recipe and to translate it so that it satisfies the particular requirements of his own restaurant. There are plenty of ideas in this book for restaurateurs to adopt or adapt to their own operation.

Miles Quest FHCIMA
Editor, *Catering Times*

*To Stephen Ross, Penny Ross
and Kenneth Bell*

Introduction

Your pig is still an apprentice at snuffing truffles. Tender-hearted, you prefer to do without foie gras rather than force feed the geese. And oh, that poor lobster whistling as you drop him live into the boiling court bouillon.

How on earth can you guarantee your survival as a restauranteur? Selling Peking duck, or maybe tagliatelli – prawn curry? But you undertake La Cuisine Françise at your peril.

Italians, Indians and Chinese, they plant their restaurants in the welcoming soil of this country and flourish. The English, at least those romantic Francophiles who open bistros, expect to adopt Gallic know-how overnight on the strength of mugging up a few cook books. What they turn out, more often than not, is a hybrid dish, sometimes good, occasionally excellent, frequently off-centre.

Economics are often to blame. Across the channel the largest proportion of the family budget passes through the alimentary canal. Paradoxically, the bistros in the back streets of York, Bristol, Birmingham and Bromsgrove have to compete with Lee Ho Yak and the local 'Trat.'.

Social status also plays its part. A good French chef, at home in his village of two or three thousand inhabitants, has a responsive, captive audience. Why should he come to this country and face the long winter evenings when the only table booked is for ten-thirty after the cinema.

In spite of this, so one hears, interest in good food has never been higher. The good food guides are instant best sellers. People collect cookery books as others collect matchboxes or butterflies.

With so much popular literature, not to mention the coverage of the mass media, there is no agreed standard of 'good food'. Given a dish of mackerel for example, a customer has a purely subjective decision to make: either he enjoys it or he does not. Hence the razamataz that one finds in some establishments: soft lights, music, slick waiters, interiors looking like film sets. They all distract from, rather than enhance, the quality of the mackerel. Yet, if one believes the consultants, 'ambiance' is an essential part of the entertainment which those eating out expect.

Given the premise that the most important thing in a restaurant is its food, it is worth considering the role of the person in front of the stove. Is he an artisan or an artist? The temptation of many aspiring chefs is to try for the latter label before mastering and understanding basic techniques. At the opposite pole there are plenty of chefs weened on the parti system whose goal is to be able to cook a tried recipe blindfold. These are the kitchen technicians, accurate, harassed and often underpaid who abound in our hotel system. Tied to their repertoire, they have little chance of developing into good chefs because they will never move outside the atmosphere in which they have been nurtured.

As in a good recipe, it is the balance of skill and flair that carries one out of the rut. Dicing an onion in five seconds flat is a useful tour de main, but it is hardly essential. To be able to smell when the pâté en croûte is cooked, is.

Were cooking as scientific as chemistry, one could pick up a recipe, work through its separate stages and finish with an identical result month after month. Up to a point many recipes are standards and have been for the last fifty years. But there will always be a margin for variety and experiment so long as cooks refuse to be stereotyped.

No recipe ever 'works' by itself without the co-operation of whoever prepares the dish. At the simplest level this means that no two people will stiffly beat egg whites alike. Both may know the trick of turning the bowl upside-down. If the white sticks to the bottom, they have been beaten enough; if not, one has to wipe the floor. Nevertheless, a differential does exist within the term 'stiffly beaten'. Stiffly beaten whites may be overbeaten in a soufflé or not beaten enough, as can occur with meringue.

Far from decrying the lack of precision, margins are what separate the journeymen from the masters.

This does not imply, as some theatrical chefs would have us think, that l'art culinaire is a gift from the gods, exclusive only to a few favoured mortals, of whom they are one. Good cooking demands good habits of preparation, good taste, dexterity and experience. In conjunction with these there has to be vision.

A few toques will shake disapprovingly at the inclusion of vision in a list of cooking skills. Unless one can foresee the end to which one is following a recipe, unless one can imagine the final taste in advance, one is unlikely to do more than a competent piece of work with the best recipe. One should read through a new recipe, disregarding the glossy illustration that may have caught the eye in the first place, relate one's cooking experience to its details and visualise how the dish is likely to turn out.

Every cook has his own style, conscious or unconscious. Some intense psychology post-graduate may at this moment be preparing a thesis on 'gustative habits and selections of the professional cook'. Whereas Chef A creates delicately balanced recipes in which all the flavours harmonise into a whole, Chef B produces dramatic contrasts equally satisfying. The former would belong to the French classical school. The latter is more likely to be a modern. Of the two the classical tradition demands first consideration on merit.

It is impossible to experiment successfully with culinary alchemy until one is familiar with the groundwork of cooking practices. There is always a tendency for any frustrated would-be artist, who by accident or design takes up cooking, to concoct various hashes. Looked at from another angle, there is always a risk that the experienced, conscientious, trained chef, bullied over his costing sheets or fighting for the survival of his own place in some cases, will cut corners and turn cowboy.

Classical standards are the foundations for anyone producing any level of French cuisine. In themselves they represent proved methods for all aspects of food production. One may adapt them by replacing Escoffier's 'brigade' with an electric blender, but their heart remains sound.

One might suppose, from the mass of regional recipes, that any generalisation of French cookery was meaningless. True, differences exist between 'haute cuisine' and 'cuisine bourgeoise', between the style of cooking in Lyons and the style of cooking in Normandy. What else would one expect in a country of such geographical diversity as France. Yet, just as the Halles at Rungis draw in the best raw materials: the best cheeses, meats, vegetables, fish and fruit to the capital from the provinces, French cooking to a large extent is centred on its classical tradition.

Bistro Style Cookery

'La Nouvelle Cuisine' in vogue in France today is really nothing of the sort. It does not strive to challenge the establishment. Rather it appears as the logical development in a constantly evolving process. What it has done, is eliminate the grotesque decoration which deformed so much food – and still does sometimes. It has opted out of menus that look more like indexes. It has extended the range of what risked becoming a stagnant repertoire. Without challenging any principles of French cookery, it aims to ensure that the amateur gastronomer does not leave the table bloated, facing the prospect of a sleepless night, paying with indigestion for his excesses at the table.

Problems for a British Bistro

The British bistro is a bit of a bastard, though its aims may be linked to those of 'La Nouvelle Cuisine'.

It is as well to clarify the limitations that will always prevent comparison with Troisgros, Bocuse and Les Prés et les Sources d'Eugénie. A little matter of twenty-two miles separates France from England. If in purely local terms we admit that a gentleman, born, bred and living in Bristol is as different from a second gentleman born, bred and living in Leeds as chalk is from the proverbial cheese, then it is evident why one cannot import wholesale a senior branch of French culture on the strength of a taste for snails and Beaujolais Nouveau.

Expertise is hard earned, especially when experience of eating French food may be limited to a fortnight's working holiday a year in the Loire valley or at St Paul de Vance, when all one's instincts are to forget one's critical objectivity in favour of uninhibited enjoyment of Gallic atmosphere.

So many good bistros are run on the enthusiasm generated by the owner, that one overlooks the shortcomings of the food. Conversely bistros have sunk without trace with the chef – patron at his ovens, to the last gallantly making his Boeuf Bourguignonne taste like the one he first ate at Dijon on his honeymoon. One fails. Another is regularly full. And why? On the strength of a friendly credit in a good food guide, a well-considered location, pretty waitresses or, in the last resort, the food.

Food has to be the prime consideration of a bistro.

Here though, one faces the second obstacle to providing authentic dishes. Nobody doubts that one can obtain first class raw materials in our markets. Yet the cost of buying the best is too often prohibitive. 'Best' needs some defining. Even today there is a division between first and second class joints of beef. Fillet steak is better than sirloin is better than rump is better than topside and so on down to the tail. Such distinction leads to the false assumption that a quality restaurant must serve fillet steak. This discounts the obvious point that each piece of beef has its own uses. The goodness depends on the preparation of the piece and its quality relative to a similar cut on another carcass. Buying the 'best' means choosing the best quality of the type of raw material one requires and paying for it.

Paying is the crux of the matter. Certain cuts of meat, certain poultry, certain game, certain fish, certain shellfish, certain vegetables have priced themselves beyond the reach of most restaurateurs. A housewife counts the pennies in her purse and decides whether she can afford to treat her family to fillet steak. The restaurateur gauges the cost, thinks of it in terms of a percentage of the selling price and decides whether his customers will be prepared to pay so much per portion.

As a result the potential bistroteur will have to reject two-thirds of a repertoire designed for the golden age of the Grand Hotel, before he begins to compose a menu. To this enforced narrowing of sights one may add the list of comestibles, commonplace in France but not generally available here: cèpes and morilles, sorrel, corn salad, to mention a few, can only be obtained from a few specialists, hence expensive sources. Hot house tomatoes which are mostly what we buy are poor cousins of the luscious, fleshy ones in French markets. Fresh herbs are in short supply. One has a constant battle obtaining interesting wet fish. Farmhouse chickens will soon be a thing of the past. Ducks have a pitiful amount of meat on them. Meat is often butchered by the butcher.

Having shown the odds stacked against the pretensions a bistro might have to serve authentic French food, it is necessary to examine the positive aspect.

The limitations can be beneficial in that they concentrate attention on the possibilities open to a resourceful chef.

If there is a single principle of good cooking, it is a refusal to compromise standards. When one cannot buy fresh scallops, one ought not make do with frozen ones. If the same fresh scallops are not up to scratch one ought not use them. There may be a few murmurs coming from the gremlins that hover over the deep freezers of this country as they read this. Unwarranted too, since certain foods may be frozen for limited periods. Sighs, too, come from the ex-idealists: 'We tried that once, but it just was not feasible'.

It is possible to disguise not-quite-up-to-scratch food with a craftily manufactured sauce. It is impossible to turn not-quite-up-to-scratch food into good food.

The case against fresh food and nothing but fresh food is that waste is tantamount to self-inflicted ruin, whereas a bistro is the last place on earth where one may accurately predict demand. Bearing in mind this attitude as another pointer, one is again focussing more closely on the number of options.

To summarise. A whole range of foods are out of the question from a cost angle. More recipes exclude themselves from want of correct ingredients. Others must be rejected because of high waste risk. What remain then are low cost dishes, carefully prepared with fresh ingredients, rigorously controlled, that may be readily obtained and which offer little risk of wastage.

Given so many predetermined factors, it might seem that scope for offering a knowledgeable customer exciting and appetising food are severely restricted. Far from it. Nor need one be reduced to ringing the changes on different garnishes for the filet de sole or the poulet sauté.

Bistro Style Cookery attempts to show how one may produce high quality French cuisine without depending on surtax clients to pay for it.

Menu making
Bistro cooking allows one to borrow freely from any branch of French techniques and dishes. This means that on the menu one may see, side by side, a potée from Brittany, a fish dish from Provence and a sweet from Auvergne. It is eclecticism of this kind which elicits the wrath of purists who believe in separating regional specialities or 'haute cuisine' from 'cuisine bourgeoise'. To which any owner may honestly reply that he is an enthusiast rather than a specialist.

Should he choose to put Bread and Butter Pudding on his menu he can please himself. An inflexible rule of what is permitted has no place in a bistro.

There is a proviso which harps back to the principle of no compromise. If one is making, say, a fish soup, one has no right to call it a Bouillabaisse because it will not be one. The fish that go to make a Bouillabaisse are not to be had from the local fishmonger. Again, if one uses hogget or mutton, it is dishonest to call it lamb. Mutton justifies itself. Its preparation will sometimes be unsuitable to lamb and vice versa.

Concocting a menu is, if anything, harder than inventing a new recipe. However much one strives to balance it, one knows in one's heart that most of those eating will plump for a Terrine de Saumon Fumé (see page 76) instead of the Terrine de Larin à la Bénédictine (see page 78). Each dish seen in detachment may seem satisfying in its own way, but detachment hardly plays a large part in the mentality of those eating out. The only answer to such a situation is to know that the Terrine de Lapin will improve if it is not eaten at once, whilst the salmon will be gobbled up before it has a chance to be over the hill.

Often shortcomings may crop up unawares. The menu that seemed fine on paper may turn up dishes which are red, red and red. It is easy to overlook colour or the over exposure of a single ingredient.

Is there an ideal length for a menu? Simply for the purpose of collating 200 recipes in this book, each core chapter has twenty-two or twenty-three recipes.

In a work context no one would hold rigidly to twenty-two recipes for six weeks, discard them and start out on twenty-two more. It would make better sense to stagger a change-over, introduce the odd dish in advance as a plat du jour, continue longer with recipes that are in most demand, phase out other dishes which fail to please the fickle public.

Nevertheless, about twenty dishes combines a fair variety for the client with a manageable amount of work for the kitchen. Ideally, from the kitchen's position, one would constantly be hoping to cut back menu length, since the shorter the menu, the more time is available to prepare each dish. The 'no choice' experiment has been tried but, with a few notable exceptions, has failed to capture the public's imagination.

Without too much over-strain, a book might have been built around the stock favourites – Boeuf Bourguignonne, Coq au Vin and Moules Marinière. By furnishing these recipes, to be found elsewhere in more authoritative sources, one would have achieved little other than to force another cook book into an already crowded market. Many of the recipes included in this book have not been printed before in this country – though of course many have.

To claim method behind what is, to some extent, a random selection would be presumptuous. However, there are causes determining the general organisation of the menus. There are no liver dishes, nor kidneys. This is not a reflection of the author's prejudices. Simply, offal is hard to shift.

When two out of nine main courses use chicken then it is because, in one instance the breasts are needed, in the other the legs. The style of each dish will be totally contrasting.

In all but one of the main course sections there are no more than two fish dishes. Firstly, fish is perishable. Secondly it is hard to sell. Some might claim that based on proportional representation two fish dishes is one too many.

Most common are the ragoûts and braised meat dishes. They can be prepared in advance of service and will improve on re-heating. It is necessary to add that one must only re-heat once.

Close examination of the body of recipes will uncover the fact that extensive use has been made of quenelles, farces and forcemeat. Without trying to defend the inclusion of a fish quenelle (one of the classics of French cookery, quick and easy to make with modern equipment), Mousseline de Poisson à la Crème de Homard (see page 237) allows a bistro to offer fresh lobster to its clientèle at less cost than a sirloin steak. Another concern behind the menu is the work load which a kitchen under pressure can face. If every dish were started when the order reached the chef, there would be chaos. Analysing the first menu, for example, two first courses and four main courses only need cooking to order. Emphasis is placed on careful preparation rather than reflex action under fire.

The opening chapter 'Doing the Basics Well' is not an exhaustive summary of cookery technique. It covers most of the methods that occur throughout the following chapters.

Maquereaux Grillés à la Moutarde, a specimen recipe from this chapter is included to illustrate the method of grilling fish and the method of making a cream reduction sauce.

Though the dependence on the classical style needs no further stressing, there is a divergence from accepted practice which will strike those who have trained in large hotels or cookery schools. There is a limited use of roux-based sauces except as part of ragoûts. The 'sauces maîtres': Demi-glace, Velouté de Poisson, Sauce de Tomates have no place. Chiefly this is because one can prepare items on a short menu individually. There is no question of ten differently named dishes sharing an identical sauce base. With most of the darker sauces a good consommé base thickened with arrowroot has been preferred to an adaptation of demi-glace. With fish sauces reductions seem to taste better, and are easier to control than heavy-handed use of a velouté.

Whether it helps to have a preparation time or not is debatable. Hopefully the margin given covers the range from novice to out-and-out professional.

Oven temperatures are given too. These tend to be like the light meter on a camera. One can vary the relationship between time and temperature according to the demands of a work situation. Though moderate, warm or hot ovens are compulsory for certain types of cooking, one may be forced into improvising a temperature which will allow two dissimilar dishes to cook side by side in the same oven. Regulos are approximate in that a professional oven is often adjusted to a higher scale of temperatures than a household oven.

Quantities given as '1 large onion', offend some readers of cookery books. Tabulating and weighing half a pound of onions (how the author sees 1 large onion) is not something that occurs in a professional environment. All relevant weights are given in metric and imperial.

Wine suggestions may help staff to steer customers in the direction of wine that will suit each dish. They are not meant as an ex-cathedra pronouncement to be followed without question. Since wine and food are yoked together, it is surprising that so little thought in this country is spent marrying good food with good wine. Someone more qualified than the author may in the future demonstrate how to make the match.

A Guide to Unit Cost

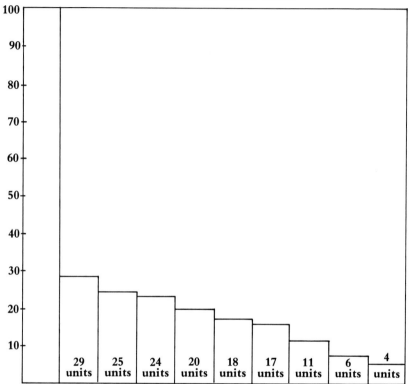

Cost price per portion using fresh raw materials.

100	Homard à l'Américaine
29	Poulet sauté au Chinon
25	Lapin à la Roquebrussanne
24	Mousseline de poisson à la crème de homard
20	Potée au pistou
18	Raie à la sauce bâtarde
17	Aillade de mouton
11	Gougères aux amandes et au jambon
6	Galette des rois
4	Soupe aux abats de porc

How to use the Unit Guide
Food prices escalate, but with the odd exception individual items tend to retain their relationship to each other. The guide is to help anyone using this book to ascertain the cost of each recipe.

There is no recipe in the book for Homard à l'Américaine. It is too costly. I have used this dish as the standard against which all other dishes have been costed. The price of lobster does indeed vary throughout the year, but the 100 units at which the dish is rated relates to when live lobsters are generally available.

If the price of Homard à l'Américaine were £1 per portion (100 units) (which it is not!), then the cost per portion of Potée au Pistou would be 20p (20 units). In general, first courses and sweets fall below 15 units. No main courses creep above 35 units.

Doing the Basics Well

Fonds de Volaille: Chicken stock
Consommé: (for use instead of beef stock)
Gelée de Viande: Meat jelly
Glace de Viande: Meat glaze
Fonds de Poisson: Fish stock
Fumet: Reduced fish stock
Glace de Poisson: Fish glaze
Poulet à l'Etuvée: Chicken stewed in butter (slow oven cooking with fats)
Ragoût de Boeuf: Beef casserole (simmering meat fully immersed in a sauce)
Queue de Boeuf Braisée: Braised oxtail (simmering meat part immersed in sauce)
Poulet Sauté Chasseur: Chicken sauté with wine, mushrooms (e.g. of chicken sauté dish)
Maquereaux Grillés à la Moutarde: Grilled mackerel with mustard sauce (grilling fish plus cream reduction sauce)
Entrecôte Grillé: Grilled sirloin
Rosbif: Roast beef
Paupiettes de Veau: Stuffed veal escalope (batting out veal plus veal stuffing)
Quenelles de Poisson: Fish dumplings (how to prepare a basic quenelle mix)
Merlan Braisé: Braised whiting (braising fish on a trivet of vegetables)
Pâté en Croûte: Pâté in pastry (handling pastry for pâtés)
Galantine de Volaille: Chicken galantine (boning out a chicken)
Sauce Hollandaise: Hollandaise sauce (basic butter compound sauce)
Sauce Madère: Madeira sauce (brown roux or arrowroot based sauce)
Feuilletage: Puff pastry

Fonds de Volaille

Chicken Stock

Amount: 2½ litres (about 4 pints). Total cost: 5 units.
Preparation: 15 mins. Cooking: 3–4 hrs.

It is fair to assume that there will always be chicken carcasses going spare in a professional kitchen. The temptation is to boil them up and forget them. Calling boiled chicken bones 'stock' is an overstatement. Still, unless one is handling large quantities of veal, chicken stock has to be an all-purpose basis for quite a few sauces. The more reason why one should take care with its preparation.

By chopping up a veal shin-bone and adding it to the stock one can make a stock which has more body than the average bouillon without destroying its character.

Ingredients   carcass, neck and giblets from 5 chickens
1 veal shin-bone
3 onions
3 carrots
2 sticks of celery
2 bayleaves
2 cloves
1 large bunch of thyme
parsley stalks
pepper

Method: Roughly chop the carcasses. Place them in a large pan with the bones.

Peel the vegetables. Add them to the pan with the herbs tied together making a bouquet garni.

Cover with cold water. Bring to the boil. Skim. Simmer for 3 to 4 hours. During the simmering, skim at regular intervals. Check that the bones are always covered with liquid. It may be necessary to top up with boiling water.

Strain the liquid into a fresh pan. Return to the boil and reduce by a third. Do not salt.

Consommé

For use instead of Beef Stock

**Amount: 5 litres (about 1 gallon). Total cost: 72 units.
Preparation: 15 mins. Cooking: 2 hrs. Other: for the beef stock
6 hrs.**

It is often adequate to have a good stock in order to make a good sauce. Using consommé is a refinement which can only justify itself in practice. It does justify itself though. Dark sauces take on a sheen and body which are impossible with 'fonds brun'.

For those who, nevertheless, consider that cost, time and energy make consommé impractical, here first is a quick way of clarifying a good stock. Beat four egg whites, mix with 3 soupspoons cooled stock and beat them into 5 litres (about 9 pints) of strained beef stock. Allow the stock to simmer for 30 minutes. Strain through a fine-meshed sieve. The method works with all stocks, meat, fish and game.

Consommé for sauces need not be as strong as it usually is for soups. Stock is used to complement a sauce, not dominate it.

Ingredients
5 litres (1 gallon) beef stock
1 kg (2¼ lb) minced, lean ox cheek
150g (5½ oz) finely chopped leek
150 g (5½ oz) finely chopped carrot
15 g (½ oz) black peppercorns
2 bayleaves
2 sprigs thyme
4 egg whites
salt

Method: Place the dry ingredients in a pan with the egg whites. Stir vigorously so the white is well mixed with the other ingredients. Pour the stock over the mixture. Bring to the boil. The mince, egg and vegetable will form a crust. Simmer very slowly for 2 hours. The crust should not be allowed to crack. Strain the consommé through muslin (a J-cloth makes a good alternative), placed over a fine-meshed sieve. Skim off any residue fat with kitchen paper.

Gelée de Viande
Meat Jelly

Amount: 1⅔ litres (about 2¾ pints). Total cost: 72 units.
Preparation: none. Cooking: 20–30 mins.

If jelly were merely for decoration one could scrap it and cooking would be no worse off. In any case the Olympian masterpieces are for kitchens which can afford a garde-manger – or the army. But meat and fish jelly do have a place in the smaller kitchen especially during long hot summers. Packet aspic is pretty unpleasant stuff. To make a good jelly, simply reduce clarified stock or consommé by two-thirds and flavour it with port, sherry or Madeira.

Glace de Viande
Meat Glaze

It is unlikely that many English restaurants are going to keep pots of meat glaze handy for finishing ragoûts and sauté dishes. But there is an exception. When making a pâté, especially a game pâté, it is a good idea to have a glaze made from the carcass. Cold food needs more seasoning than hot food anyway.

To make a glaze is easy. After the basic stock has been clarified, continue reducing. A pint of game stock, for example, will give a couple of soupspoons of glaze.

Fonds de Poisson
Fish Stock

Amount: 2½ litres (about 4 pints). Total cost: 5 units.
Preparation: 15 mins. Cooking: 30 mins.

At college one learns that sole, whiting, turbot and brill bones and trimmings make the best fish stock. To this list one can add salmon and, to a lesser extent, trout.

There is no strict rule as to what one may put in a fish stock, but a pound of trimmings will give a pint of good fish stock. The most readily available trimmings are whiting heads which most fishmongers will be only too happy to supply.

Ingredients
2¼ kg (about 5 lb) fish bones and trimmings
1 lemon zest and juice
150 g (5½ oz) onions
150 g (5½ oz) celery tops
500 ml (17 fl oz) dry white wine
thyme
1 bayleaf
fennel
parsley stalks
white peppercorns
sea salt (optional)

Method: Dice the vegetables and put them in a large saucepan. Add the herbs, spices and lemon. Place the fish bones and trimmings on top. Moisten with 2½ litres water (about 5 pints) and half a litre (17 fl oz) of dry white wine. Bring to the boil. Skim. Simmer for 30 minutes. Strain.

Whether one adds salt to the stock is again a matter of taste. If it is to be used for poaching i.e. as a court bouillon, it can be seasoned immediately with a little less than half an ounce of sea salt. However, if the stock is to be used in a reduction, it is better left unseasoned or there is a real risk of the dish being too salty.

Fumet
Reduced Fish Stock

Amount: 1¼ litres. Total cost: 5 units. Preparation: 10 mins. Cooking: reduction 15 mins, simmering 20 mins.

When one reduces a fish stock by about a half it becomes 'fumet'. Cooled, it will set to a jelly. First though, clarify the 'fumet' with three egg whites beaten into the stock. Simmer for 20 minutes with the egg whites and pass through a sieve.

Glace de Poisson
Fish Glaze

If one is not going to use a basic fish velouté for fish sauces it facilitates the reduction if one uses a ready-made glaze. Once the 'fumet' has been clarified, continue reducing till about 2 fl oz per pint (75 ml per 550 ml) is left.

Poulet à l'Etuvée
Chicken Stewed in Butter

Serves: 8. Total cost: 24 units. Preparation: 20–30 mins. Cooking: 1½ hrs. Oven: 140°C/310°F/Gas Mk 2. Wine suggestion: Bordeaux – St Emilion

Bistro Style Cookery

Ingredients   2 medium chickens cut into 16 pieces
4 large onions
2 leeks
1 large carrot
2 cloves garlic
160 g (5 ½ oz) butter
75 ml (2 fl oz) groundnut oil
1 sprig thyme
350 ml (10 fl oz) double cream
100 ml (3 ½ fl oz) cognac
450 g (1 lb) mushrooms
1 lemon
salt and pepper

Method: Put three-quarters of the oil and butter in a heavy-duty ovenproof dish. Slice the onion, leek and carrot. Place them in the dish. Arrange the pieces of chicken on top (breasts and legs separate). Add the sprig of thyme and the garlic. Season. Cover. Place the dish in a low temperature oven. After one hour, remove the lid and moisten with cognac. Replace in oven and continue cooking for 30 minutes more.

Sauté the mushrooms in the rest of the oil, butter and juice of a lemon. Season. Add to the chicken. Strain off any excess fat. Pour the cream over the chicken. Heat rapidly until the cream thickens.

Note: Chicken breasts cook faster than the legs. To make the dish perfect remove the breasts from the ovenproof dish after 45 minutes and return them to it for the last 15 minutes.

To Bone a Chicken for Sauté or Etuvée Dishes

(a) Pull one leg away from carcass and slit loose skin.
(b) Using the tip of the knife, cut around the nut of meat in the back.
(c) Pull back the leg sharply against the joint to dislocate the thigh bone.
(d) Again with the tip of the knife free the leg from the carcass.
(e) Cut the leg into two between the drumstick and the thigh.
(f) Repeat the five sections above with the second leg.
(g) Scrape along the inside of the wish-bone and pull it free from the carcass.
(h) With the tip of the knife, free one breast from carcass.
(i) Divide the breasts.
(j) Free the breast from the carcass, cutting through the wing joint.
(k) Cut the breast into two pieces, one of which is still attached to the wing.
(l) Repeat the above with the second breast ((i) is of course superfluous now).

26

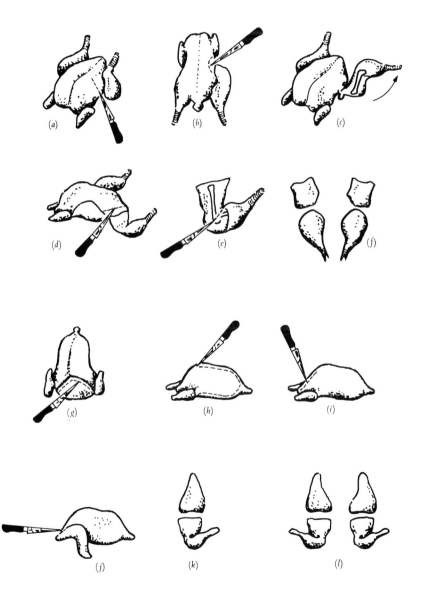

Ragoût de Boeuf
Beef Casserole

Serves: 8. Total cost: 20 units. Preparation: 20–30 mins. Cooking: 1½ hrs. Wine suggestion: Mâcon Rouge, Santenay.

Ingredients
1350 g (about 3 lb) chuck-steak
3 onions
4 cloves garlic
100 ml (3¾ fl oz) groundnut oil or the same amount of beef dripping
50 g (scant 2 oz) tomato purée
80 g (3 oz) flour
400 ml (14 fl oz) red wine
400 ml (14 fl oz) consommé
2 bayleaves
thyme
50 g (scant 2 oz) sugar
salt and pepper

Method: Cube the beef into 50 gm (2 oz) pieces. Heat the oil till it almost smokes. Fry the beef a few pieces at a time in the oil, transferring the pieces to a dish as they brown. Sprinkle sugar on the beef while in the pan. It helps with the browning. Next fry the onions and garlic till they are well coloured. Deglaze the pan with a little wine or consommé. Return the meat to the pan. Stir in flour and then tomato purée. Allow to brown. Pour in the wine and consommé a third at a time. Add the salt, pepper and herbs. Simmer for 1½ hours. Top up with extra consommé if necessary.

Note: This basic beef stew can be turned into a Boeuf à la Bourguignonne, by adding lardons, mushrooms and button onions;

The reason for frying the meat only a few pieces at a time is that if one puts too many pieces in the pan, the temperature of the oil or fat lowers and the meat will stew instead of brown.

It may be necessary, if the meat is fatty, to drain off some of the excess fat before deglazing the pan.

Queue de Boeuf Braisée
Braised Oxtail

Serves: 8. Total cost: 16 units. Preparation: 20–30 mins. Cooking: 4 hrs. Other: soaking 2 hrs. Wine suggestion: Red V.D.Q.S. e.g. Corbières, Costières du Gard.

The basic difference between a braised meat and a ragoût is the quantity of liquid that is used. Theoretically, the meat is only partly covered for braising. The other technicality is that one usually places the meat on a bed of vegetables. Though this is a good idea with some cuts of beef, say for a carbonnade, it is not necessary for oxtail. The cooking time is so long, about 4 hours, that the vegetables would long have become uninteresting. The other difficulty which oxtail presents is the quantity of fat that seeps into the sauce. One can, of course, skim off most of it with absorbent kitchen paper. It is probably better to leave the dish a day after cooking. The fat will have set and be easy to remove. Besides the dish, like most stews, is better for re-heating.

Ingredients 1350 g (3 lb) oxtail
450 g (1 lb) belly of pork
600 ml (1 pint) red wine
80 g (3 oz) flour
30 g (1 oz) brown sugar
30 g (1 oz) tomato purée
450 g (1 lb) mirepoix of carrot, onion and celery
4 cloves
bouquet garni
beef stock or consommé
salt and pepper

Method: Soak the oxtail for 2 hours in cold water. Brown the pieces, plus the belly of pork in a large pan without oil if possible, though it may be necessary to brush a little on the bottom of the pan. Stir in the flour. Let it brown. Add the tomato purée and wine. It will be necessary to add stock, but the quantity depends on the size of the pan. The meat should be two-thirds covered. Add the cloves, bouquet garni and some seasoning. Cover and allow to simmer very gently for 2 hours, topping up with stock as necessary.

Now add the rough dice of vegetables. Turn over the meat. Cover and simmer for a further 2 hours, still topping up with stock.

Note: The brown sugar is an optional extra. It sweetens obviously, but it helps to give a shine to the sauce as well as balancing the strong flavour of the cloves. Add it when the vegetables are added to the pan.

Poulet Sauté Chasseur
Chicken Sauté with Wine and Mushrooms

Serves: 8. Total cost: 20 units. Preparation: 20–30 mins. Cooking: sauce 30 mins, meat 12 mins. Wine suggestion: Bordeaux – Pomerol or Beaujolais – Brouilly.

Just one of the many poulet sauté dishes in the répertoire, along with the others, it is often massacred by demi-glaze and culinary malpractice.

The first thing to remember about a sauté dish is that one ought never to boil it in the accompanying sauce. Chicken will toughen and overcook if one simmers it in the sauce after it has been sautéd.

Next, the times are critical. The white meat only takes 7 or 8 minutes cooking, but the legs need an additional 4 or 5 minutes.

Ingredients
    2 medium chickens
    400 g (14 oz) Italian tomatoes
    350 g (12–13 oz) button mushrooms
    2 shallots
    600 ml (1 pint) chicken stock
    300 ml (10 fl oz) white wine
    1 soupspoon arrowroot
    1 soupspoon cognac
    60 g (2 oz) butter
    75 ml (2½ fl oz) groundnut oil
    tarragon
    salt and pepper

Method: Dissolve the arrowroot in a little stock. Heat the remainder of the stock. Pass the tomatoes on to the stock. (Tinned tomatoes provide better flavour than hot house varieties, but if good fresh tomatoes are available then use them.) Allow to simmer. Bind with the arrowroot.

Heat the butter and oil. Place the seasoned pieces of chicken (16 – made up of 8 pieces of breast and 8 of leg) skin down in the oil. Colour thoroughly. Turn.

Slice the mushrooms. When the breast meat is cooked, remove and keep warm (but not in an oven where it will dry out). Add the mushrooms to the pan. As soon as the legs are cooked place them with the breasts.

Deglaze the pan with the white wine. Add the finely diced shallots and stock to which the tomato has been added. Add two sprigs of fresh tarragon to the pan. Reduce to a coating consistency. Check seasoning. Remove from heat. Return the chicken pieces to the pan for 2 minutes. Finish by adding cognac and arrange on a serving dish.

Note: If fresh tarragon is out of season, soak some dried tarragon in a little vinegar and let it cook out in the simmering stock.

Maquereaux Grillés à la Moutarde
Grilled Mackerel with Mustard Sauce

Serves: 8. Total cost: 10 units. Preparation: 5–10 mins. Cooking: fish 6-8 mins, sauce 10 mins. Wine suggestion: any Sauvignon.

Grilling fish, whether under the salamander or on the grill with the heat underneath, has its basic rules. One, dry the fish thoroughly before oiling and grilling. Two, use as high a temperature as possible.

To anyone who has passed his City & Guilds exams, mustard sauce equals béchamel with mustard added. So it is. But try making it as a reduction. The sauce is lighter, better flavoured and just as easy to make. If one thinks about it, a béchamel is really unsuitable for any fish sauce, weighing down something that is delicately flavoured.

Ingredients   8 smallish mackerel
50 ml (1¾ fl oz) groundnut oil
salt and pepper
For the sauce:
100 ml (3½ fl oz) fumet
100 ml (3½ fl oz) white wine
1 soupspoon Dijon mustard
225 ml (8 fl oz) double cream
salt and pepper

Method: Dry the mackerel. Season them inside and out. Brush with oil on both sides. Place on the grill, about 4 minutes each side.

In a pan reduce the wine and fumet by about half. Stir in the mustard. Add the cream and reduce till it thickens to a coating consistency. Check the seasoning. Pour over the mackerel.

Entrecôte Grillée

Grilled Sirloin

Serves: 1. Total cost: 30 units. Preparation: 35–45 mins per whole sirloin. Cooking: depending on whether rare, medium etc. Wine suggestion: Burgundy.

How long should one grill a steak? A 200 g (7 oz) portion is plenty. The time in minutes will depend on the heat of the grill. However, for a blue steak, one should grill the meat for 1 minute on each side and turn down the temperature of the grill so that the meat heats right the way through. For any other steaks, rare, medium, well-done, oil and use a hot grill throughout. There is an exception. If someone wants a really well-done steak, finish cooking in the oven or he will end up with a burnt offering.

There are a number of tips for good steak making. Do not grill meat straight out of the refrigerator – let it stand at room temperature for at least half an hour. Remove all nerves and tendons when preparing the meat. They cause shrinkage in grilling. Score the edges of an entrecôte to prevent the edges from turning up. Do not salt till after grilling or the blood will sweat. It is also unwise to prick a steak to see how it is cooked. One can usually tell by pressing the meat with one's finger; one washes one's hands before and after this operation!

In an article written for *Catering Times,* the author once suggested that there was a case for using a special grilling oil. Perhaps he was putting the cart before the horse. First priority is a good quality sunflower or groundnut oil. Once one has an oil which is tasteless, one can think in terms of playing around with flavours.

To prepare a grilling oil, one has a margin for personal preference. But certain herbs suit grilled meat better. The chief one is thyme. So one starts by adding a couple of good sprigs of fresh thyme to 500 ml (17½ fl oz) oil. Next one may add rosemary, bayleaves and a leaf or two of sage. A commercial French oil uses grape pips. Leave the oil to macerate for several days before use so that the flavour of the herbs can develop.

Rosbif
Roast Beef

**Total cost: 30 units. Preparation: 35–45 mins per whole sirloin.
Cooking: 15 mins plus 10–15 mins per 450 g (1 lb). Oven:
235°C/455°F/Gas Mk 8. Wine suggestion: Burgundy – Volnay.**

Preparing joints of sirloin for the oven begins where the butcher's work
ends. His percentage comes in selling as much of the fat around the
sirloin itself as is compatible with fair trading. The cook's job is to trim
excess fat, remove nerves and filaments and tie the joints so the meat
may be cooked under the best possible conditions.

Trim away most of the surface fat, leaving only a 6 mm (¼ in) strip
covering the sirloin itself. Using the tip of a knife lift this piece of fat
from the meat leaving it attached to the bottom corner. Again using the
point of the knife remove all the nerves and filaments adhering to the
meat, taking care not to cut into the flesh. These nerves are elastic and
cause the meat to shrink during roasting. Pull the trimmed fat back over
the meat. Divide the sirloin into joints for two, four or six people. Now
tie the joints with kitchen string. Rub with a little butter. Pepper. Place
the joint on a cooling rack over a roasting tin. Place, in a hot oven.
Roast for 15 minutes, plus about 10 minutes per 450 g (1 lb) for rare
meat, 15 minutes per 450 g (1 lb) for beef that will be quite pink in the
middle.

To make the sauce, slice a few mushrooms. Drop them in the roasting
tin. Deglaze the tin with a tablespoon of brandy. Whisk in a little cream
and season.

Note: Let the joint settle from 5 to 20 minutes according to size before
carving. Turn the joint during this time to obtain even distribution of
the juices.

Paupiettes de Veau
Stuffed Veal Escalope

**Serves: 8. Total cost: 24 units. Preparation: 40–50 mins. Cooking:
20 mins, sauce 10 mins. Other: chilling 1 hr. Oven:
200°C/392°F/Gas Mk 6. Wine suggestion: red Beaujolais; white
Meursault.**

---

c

It is possible to flatten an escalope of veal weighing less than 112 g (4 oz) so that it fills a large plate, which is exactly what thousands of restaurants do.

Paupiettes, in so far as one only needs 112 g (4 oz) escalopes, are no exception but they offer far more scope than, say a Wiener-Schnitzel. The stuffing is all important. The recipe below is for a forcemeat made with veal sweetbreads. It is delicate and in complete contrast to the pungent oregano or rosemary with which Italians season veal. But it would be foolish to be dogmatic and claim that there is only one stuffing for veal. Every chef will discover his own preference.

In the past, it was usual to braise paupiettes and prepare the sauce with the braising stock. The advent of foil and cooking films allows us to bake escalopes 'en papillote' and they taste better for it. Any juices which the paupiettes sweat during cooking will be added to the sauce.

Ingredients   16 × 55 g (2 oz) veal escalopes
80 g (3 oz) butter
salt and pepper
For the farce:
450 g (1 lb) veal sweetbreads
3 egg whites
150 ml (5 fl oz) double cream
2 slices stale white bread
2 teaspoons sage
1 teaspoon nutmeg
salt and pepper
(milk)
For the sauce:
300 ml (10 fl oz) chicken stock
100 ml (3½ fl oz) cream
½ lemon
2 yolks
salt and pepper

Method: Tap out the escalopes with a cutlet bat, making them as square as possible.

Poach the sweetbreads 10 minutes in boiling, salted water. Drain. Clean. Blend them in a liquidiser. Season with sage, nutmeg, a level teaspoon salt and half a teaspoon white pepper.

Soak bread, without crusts, in milk. Squeeze out as much moisture as possible. Add to the veal and blend thoroughly. Now, blend in the egg whites. Chill.

Blend in the cream (it should have just come from the fridge too). Spread a soupspoon of the forcemeat on to each escalope. Wrap like parcels. Tie with kitchen string. Butter a large sheet of foil. Place the paupiettes in two or three rows on the foil. Dot each escalope with butter. Seal the foil. Bake in a hottish oven 20 minutes.

Reduce the stock by two-thirds. Add the juices rendered from the paupiettes and lemon juice. Add the cream. Check the seasoning. Bind the sauce with the yolks.

Cut the strings around the paupiettes. Coat with the sauce.

Quenelles de Poisson
Fish Dumplings

Serves: 8. Total cost: 8 units. Preparation: 10–15 mins. Cooking: 10 mins. Other: to chill 1 hr. Wine suggestion: Chablis.

Before electrical appliances took a hold in the modern kitchen quenelles used to be one of the mystic dishes that went under the label 'haute cuisine'. What with the pounding and the whisking above ice, all to make a light dumpling, the task hardly seemed worth it unless one had a battery of commis on hand. From the point of view both of flavour and texture quenelles are still a delicacy, but they are neither time-consuming nor expensive to make. They are perfectly adapted to some of the high quality sauces which appear later in the book, when their relative cheapness offsets the cost and labour of the sauce.

Ingredients   450 g (1 lb) whiting fillets
4 slices stale white bread
5 egg whites
350 ml (12 fl oz) double cream
grated zest of a lemon
1 level teaspoon nutmeg
1 level teaspoon white pepper
1 heaped teaspoon salt
fumet
a little milk

Method: Blend the fish to a purée in the liquidiser. Season with salt, pepper, nutmeg and finely grated zest. Soak the bread in milk. Squeeze out as much moisture as possible. Add to the fish and blend well. Repeat the process with the egg whites. Place in the coldest part of the fridge for 1 hour, at least.

Add the cream (it should have just come from the fridge, too) to the fish. Blend well till the mixture has formed a smooth, manageable paste.

Shape the quenelle mixture cigar fashion, using two tablespoons dipped in hot water. Drop each quenelle into simmering fumet, a little on the salty side. Poach until the quenelles puff. Drain on kitchen paper and serve as soon as possible

Merlan Braisé
Braised Whiting

Serves: 8. Total cost: 12 units. Preparation: 15–20 mins. Cooking: 20 mins. Oven: 190°C/374°F/Gas Mk 5. Wine suggestion: Muscadet.

Ingredients   8 medium (or 4 large) whiting
200 g (7 oz) celery
200 g (7 oz) leeks
200 g (7 oz) onions
200 g (7 oz) carrots
80 g (3 oz) butter
300 ml (10 fl oz) fish stock
thyme
fennel
salt and pepper

Method: Fillet the whiting and keep the heads and bones for fish stock. Season the fillets and sprinkle with a little chopped fennel. Place the pairs of fillets together.

Finely chop (brunoise dice) the vegetables. Place them in a pan with the butter. Add thyme and seasoning. Cover. Allow to sweat for 10 minutes.

Place the pairs of fillets on the bed of vegetables. Pour over the stock. Bring to the boil. Cover. Place in a moderate oven for 20 minutes.

Note: Whiting as a fish is underrated in this country. It is both delicately flavoured and digestible. As with most round fish it has to be quite fresh or the flavour degenerates to an unpleasant, anonymous fishiness.

Pâté en Croûte
Pâté in Pastry

Serves: 10. Total cost: 8 units. Preparation: 40–50 mins. Cooking: 1½ hrs. Other: for marinading 12 hours. Oven: 15 mins at 235°C/455°F/Gas Mk 8, 1¼ hrs at 175°C/347°F/Gas Mk 4.

Unlike a sauce which one can adjust, pâté en croûte cannot be 'doctored'. Once the farce is wrapped in the paste and committed to the oven, that's that.

Easiest to make is the farce, however. Whether one uses a pork, poultry or game filling it is necessary to bear a few things in mind. First, the pâté will taste better if the ingredients are allowed to marinade overnight. Even 12 hours is only just long enough. Cut a piece of chicken breast in half that has been in a marinade and one finds that the marinade has barely penetrated the flesh. Second, chopping the meat is better than mincing and mincing is better than blending in a large commercial liquidiser. The latter is only useful for liver pâtés and mousses. Thirdly, the seasoning and spicing are of prime importance. The first pâtés which I made for French friends were described as: 'pas assez relevés', not seasoned enough. Cold food inevitably needs that bit more salt, pepper, herbs and spices.

It is not only in England that raised pie dishes are hard to come by. The reason is obvious. Outside a few restaurants nobody takes the trouble to make pâté en croûte. In England we have a tradition of veal and ham pies and pork pies, but these are made with an indigestible hot water crust paste, rolled twice as thick as necessary. Providing that one rolls it correctly an ordinary rich shortcrust paste is ideal for this dish – and it's edible. A useful tip is to roll the pastry for the top a little thicker than for the base and sides to prevent cracking.

One may need about 300 ml (10 fl oz) of jelly to finish the pâté en croûte. It gives the moisture in the same way that a sauce or gravy is used.

Bistro Style Cookery

Ingredients *For the farce:*
450 g (1 lb) stewing veal
250 g (9 oz) smoked bacon
200 g (7 oz) minced belly of pork
2 shallots
1 large egg
100 ml (3½ fl oz) white wine
sage
thyme
2 bayleaves
1 heaped teaspoon allspice
3 cloves garlic
salt and pepper
For the paste:
350 g (12 oz) flour
200 g (7 oz) butter
2 eggs
melted butter
1 yolk for glaze
For the jelly:
300 ml (10 fl oz) gelée de viande (page 23)

Method: Chop the stewing veal and bacon. Mince the shallots and garlic. Prepare a marinade with shallots, garlic, white wine, sage, thyme, bayleaves (fresh, or use 3 dried bayleaves), allspice, salt and pepper. Place the meats in the marinade and leave overnight. Drain off a little of the wine. Lightly beat the egg and mix into the meats and marinade.

Make a pâte brisée. Crumb the flour and butter. Add the whole eggs together and work them into the flour. Do not over-knead the paste or it will toughen. Rest for 20 minutes.

Butter a raised pie dish. Roll out two-thirds of the paste and line the dish. Take care there are no creases or the paste will split. Spread the farce to fill the dish. Roll out the remainder of the paste. Water the edges and place the top on the dish. Make a hole, about the size of a ten penny piece in the top. Roll a thick piece of paste to make a chimney. Water the edge around the hole and fix the chimney in place.

Beat the yolk with a splash of water. Brush this glaze over the top. Place in a hot oven 15 minutes to set the pastry. Turn the heat right down to 175°C/347°F/Gas Mk 4 and bake for about 1¼ hours more. Cool.

Pour the jelly through the chimney just before it starts to set and while the inside of the pâté is still a little warm.

Galantine de Volaille
Chicken Galantine

Preparation: boning 15–30 mins.

Note: Galantine recipe page 182.

The galantine made to Carême's recipe is perhaps out of reach of most restaurants where cost and time available for preparation are limited. It is unlikely that one may aspire to the window dressing of Fauchon, the famous delicatessen in Place de la Madeleine. What we are bound to do is to cut one's coat according to our circumstances.

That said, there is no need to produce a second-rate piece of work. One may suppress the tongue, truffle and foie gras, one may not feel inclined to spend hours, dressing the galantine in chaud-froid underwear and aspic uniform, but one can furnish an attractive and, more important, well-flavoured first course.

There are alternative ways of proceeding in a modern kitchen. Once the galantine has been stuffed either one wraps it in cloth and poaches it in wine and chicken stock or one wraps it in buttered foil and bakes it in the oven. In the latter case, one tries to fashion the chicken as close to its former shape as possible.

The farce used is going to be chicken based, but will depend to a certain extent on personal taste providing one bears in mind that chicken is delicately flavoured. For example, you might add a little curry powder to a galantine, but curry powder dominated galantine would be unacceptable.

Boning out the chicken is likely to cause the most difficulty because one must not damage the skin.

Place the chicken so its breast is down on the preparation surface. Cut the skin along the length of the backbone. Remove the 'parson's nose'. Using the tip of a sharp knife free the thigh bones and oysters of meat along the back from the carcass. Free the wings from their joints on the carcass. Following the contour of the carcass with the point of the knife ease off the breasts. Remove the carcass.

Cut the skin around the joints at the ends of the thighbones and wings. Pull the legs and then the wings free from the skin. Take care not to tear the skin. Again use the point of the knife, if necessary, to free the flesh. The breasts should pull away from the skin without difficulty.

If one is going to poach the galantine as opposed to baking it, soak the skin in cold water while preparing the farce. You will be left with the two legs to bone and also the wings. This method of boning is applicable to the Ballottine de Caneton recipe on page 57, and the Dodine de Pintade on page 242.

Sauce Hollandaise
Hollandaise Sauce

Serves: 10 approx. Total cost: 30 units. Preparation: 10–15 mins. Cooking: during preparation.

Butter compound sauces, and Hollandaise is the basic one, are more versatile than many people might think. Apart from Béarnaise, Hollandaise with a reduction of tarragon, vinegar, peppercorns and a little bayleaf, which is quite common, one can make a sauce Choron – Hollandaise plus tomato concentrate, a mixture of Hollandaise with ground pistachio nuts, or add a little reduced fish stock and garlic to Hollandaise as an accompaniment for Bourride.

Hollandaise often lurks around the bain-marie during the whole of a work session. To avoid the embarrassment of it turning at a crucial moment, one can place it in the liquidiser, blend it (the effect is of a double emulsion) and thin it a little with boiling water. The sauce is then almost separation proof and has a smoother texture.

If one does not want to go to the trouble of enriching a fish sauce by whisking in butter, 'monter au beurre', add a little Hollandaise to the sauce at the last moment.

Ingredients   5 yolks
500 g (17–18 oz) clarified butter
mustard
wine vinegar
lemon juice
salt and pepper

Method: Place the yolks in the top half of a double saucepan or in a bowl over a bain-marie. Season with salt and pepper. Add a teaspoon of Dijon mustard. Whisk together. Now whisk in a little of the butter (it should be quite hot so the eggs cook) till the mixture emulsifies. Add a little wine vinegar. Whisk in the rest of the butter (one can add about half a small ladle-full at a time) adding the rest of the wine vinegar and lemon juice to taste.

Note: Because there is always a risk of separation if the sauce becomes too hot or too cool, it is worth keeping a little boiling water handy. One can bring back a turned sauce by whisking in a little if one is quick enough.

Sauce Madère

Madeira Sauce

Serves: 16 approx. Total cost: 96 units. Preparation: 15–20 mins. Cooking: 1 hr.

Madeira sauce is a sauce with Madeira in it. Obviously! That said one must add that there is no single 'right' way of making a Sauce Madère. Standard practice is to splash a little Madeira into demi-glace. This presupposes that one has a pot of demi-glace which will be used for half a dozen other brown sauces. It is worth asking oneself what one expects from a brown sauce – body, texture, colour.

By body – a sauce rich in flavour, yet digestible. By texture – a sauce which will coat without clogging. By colour – a sauce which provides a satisfying complement to meats which it accompanies.

One is left with alternatives. Either one thickens some consommé with arrowroot or fécule or one builds up a brown sauce from scratch. The following is a recipe for the latter method.

Ingredients   160 g (6 oz) butter
160 g (6 oz) flour
80 g (3 oz) carrot
80 g (3 oz) onion
80 g (3 oz) celery
2¼ litres (about 5 pints) consommé (see page 22)
500 ml (15 fl oz) red wine
1 bayleaf
salt and pepper
200 ml (7 fl oz) Madeira

Method: Make a dark brown roux with the butter and flour. You need to do this slowly or the flour is likely to burn or cook unevenly.

Finely dice the vegetables. Stir into the roux. Remove the pan from the heat and allow to cool slightly. Add a third of the consommé and return to the heat. Boil. Add the rest of the consommé and red wine. Season with pepper and bayleaf. Simmer for at least 1 hour till the sauce is well reduced and a shade thick. Check the seasoning. (Do not pass the sauce.) Whisk in the Madeira just before serving.

Note: It is better not to let the Madeira boil in the sauce.

The sauce will have a better shine if a little caramel is added to it during the simmering stage.

Feuilletage
Puff Pastry

Amount: 3 kg (6¾ lb). Total cost: 70 units. Preparation: 45–60 mins.

On the assumption that puff pastry is a time-consuming process, many cooks succumb to the temptation of the frozen product, which puffs effectively and is ready for immediate use. Such an attitude reduces one of the tastiest elements in pâtisserie to the role of decoration.

The difficulty of making puff pastry lies not in its stop-go stages, nor in the price tag. What only comes with practice is the 'feel' of the paste. There used to be a rule of thumb that in summer one added iced water and in winter tepid. Without being dogmatic either about method (there are three basic ones) or quantities, one wants a paste which remains supple and is easy to roll without exerting pressure on the rolling pin. Also one wants to keep the butter at a malleable temperature without letting it become too soft or too hard.

Ingredients   about 1·4 kg (a little over 3 lb) flour
1·2 kg (2¾ lb) salted butter
550 ml (1 pint) water
125 ml (5 fl oz) white wine vinegar

Method: Crumb a third of the butter with the flour (preferably strong flour). Mix the wine vinegar and water. Mix to a soft but elastic paste with the flour. Roll out this paste so it forms an oblong about 1¼ cm (½ in) thick. Either by hand, or between two sheets of grease-proof paper, flatten the rest of the butter. Its shape should be two-thirds the length of the oblong and a little less than the width. Place the butter at one end of the paste (fig 1). Fold the flap of paste uncovered by the butter, back over the butter. Now fold the paste over again so it completely encases the butter. The effect is of a flattened Swiss Roll (fig 2).

Flour the work surface. Place the paste, folds towards you. The bottom flap should rest on the work surface. Roll out till the paste reverts to its original size. Fold in three. Rest for 15 minutes. Repeat five times more. Each time the 'Swiss Roll' should be facing you before rolling.

Each rolling is called a turn (figs. 3a, 3b, 3c) because the folded paste has to turn through 90° each time in order to be facing you.

Sequence for making Feuilletage (Puff Pastry)

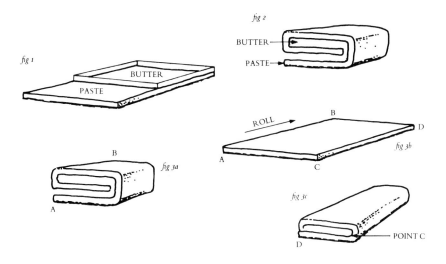

Menu 1

January–February

First Courses
page 47

Main Courses
page 55

Sweets
page 66

First Courses

Soufflé de Sole au Noilly
Dover Sole Soufflé with Noilly Prat

Serves: 8. Total cost: 16 units. Preparation: 15–25 mins. Cooking: 10–12 mins. Oven: 235°C/455°F/Gas Mk 8. Wine suggestion: Pouilly Fumé.

Ingredients   8 fillets of Dover sole
200 ml (7 fl oz) béchamel or thickened fish stock
5 yolks
6 egg whites
½ coffeespoon mace
50 ml (1¾ fl oz) Noilly Prat
75 g (scant 3 oz) butter
salt and a pinch of cayenne pepper

Method: Butter and flour eight small, individual soufflé dishes. Place them in the freezer for an hour. Gently sauté the fillets in the remaining butter. Blend them in the liquidiser with the Noilly Prat. Mix this purée with béchamel or the fish velouté, mace and yolks. Season generously to overcome the blandness of the whites. Beat the whites till the peaks are stiff. Beat a little of the whites into the mixture. Fold in the remainder with a metal spoon. Spoon enough mixture into each soufflé dish to all but fill. Bake in a hot oven, 10 to 12 minutes.

Note: If one wants the soufflé to rise evenly, smooth the filling with a palette knife before putting in the oven. Ease the mixture away from the edge of the soufflé dish with a knife.

To avoid the risk of collapse, add a little baking powder to the mixture before folding in the whites or prick them with a needle when they come out of oven.

Pâté de Champignons
Mushroom Pâté with Apples and Cognac

Serves: 8. Total cost: 7 units. Preparation: 15–20 mins. Cooking: 15 mins. Other: 2 hrs to set the pâté. Wine suggestion: Red V.D.Q.S. e.g. Corbières.

Ingredients   500 g (18 oz) mushrooms
                    250 g (9 oz) streaky bacon
                    2 apples
                    60 g (2 oz) shallots
                    110 g (4 oz) butter
                    1 pinch nutmeg
                    2 soupspoons cognac
                    salt and pepper

Method: Dice the bacon. Fry till crisp. Drain. Set aside. Add half the butter to the fat rendered by the bacon. Chop mushrooms and shallots. Peel, core and grate apples (eaters). Sweat the apple, shallots and mushrooms in the fat for 15 minutes. Season with nutmeg, salt and pepper. Melt remaining butter. Transfer the contents of the pan to the liquidiser. Add melted butter and cognac. Blend to a purée.

Spoon into individual ramekins or cassolettes, or else tartlets of shortcrust pastry. Serve with toast.

Note: The butter content will set the pâté. One may stiffen or soften the texture by adding or subtracting from it.

Soupe de Poisson
Fish Soup

Serves: 8. Total cost: 13 units. Preparation: 15–25 mins. Cooking: 2 hrs. Other: 24 hrs before re-heating. Wine suggestion: Hermitage blanc.

Ingredients   700 g (1 ½ lb) whiting fillets
                    100 g (3 ½ oz) carrots
                    100 g (3 ½ oz) celery
                    100 g (3 ½ oz) onion
                    4–6 cloves garlic
                    1 medium tin (about 1 lb) Italian tomatoes
                    700 ml (1¼ pints) fish stock
                    500 ml (17 fl oz) dry white wine
                    75 ml (2 ½ fl oz) olive oil
                    fennel, parsley, dill
                    1 pinch saffron
                    sea salt and pepper

D

Method: Finely chop the vegetables. Sweat them in the heated olive oil. Add liquidised tomatoes, stock and wine, seasoning with chopped herbs, sea salt and pepper. Allow to simmer for 2 hours. Cut the fish into pieces, add to the soup and remove pan from heat. Stir in saffron. Leave to stand overnight before using. The soup is much improved by re-heating.

Note: Take care not to re-boil the soup often or the fish will crumble.

One can add other fish according to taste e.g. a hint of smoked mackerel, mussels etc.

If there is a little quenelle mixture spare in the kitchen, one may poach a few teaspoon sized dumplings in the soup before serving.

Beignets de Cervelles
Brain Fritters with a Gribiche Sauce

Serves: 8. Total cost: 16 units. Preparation: 35–45 mins. Cooking: brains 20 mins, frying 5 mins, sauce 10–15 mins. Other: soaking brains 2 hrs, batter 1 hr. Wine suggestion: Mâcon blanc.

Ingredients   4 sets of sheep's brains
1 lemon
300 ml (about 10 fl oz) chicken stock
thyme
salt and pepper
For the batter:
110 g (4 oz) flour
25 g (scant 1 oz) butter
1 soupspoon brandy
2 egg whites
salt and pepper
(warm water)

Method: Prepare a batter. Melt the butter. Add enough warm water to the flour to make a paste the texture of heavy cream. Mix in the butter and brandy. Season. Fold in stiffly beaten whites. Rest for 1 hour.

Soak the brains in cold water for 2 hours. Rinse. Squeeze the juice of a lemon into the boiling stock. Add a good sprig of thyme, salt and pepper. Poach the brains 20 minutes. Drain. Wipe. Slice into medallions, about five per portion. Dip each piece of brain in the batter with sugar tongs. Deep-fry for 5 minutes.

Sauce for Beignets

Ingredients   4 hardboiled yolks
250 ml (9 fl oz) groundnut oil
1 teaspoon Dijon mustard
1 pinch mustard powder
juice of half a lemon
1 teaspoon chopped capers
salt and pepper

Method: Blend the yolks, mustards and lemon juice in the liquidiser. Add a little of the oil. Blend till it emulsifies. Add more oil and repeat until all the oil is incorporated. (Keep a little boiling water to hand to prevent the emulsion becoming too stiff.) Season. Stir in capers.

Note: This sauce is smoother and more digestible than a conventional tartare sauce made with mayonnaise, but needs careful handling or it separates.

Soupe aux Abats de Porc

Pork and Split Pea Soup

Serves: 8. Total cost: 4 units. Preparation: 20–30 mins. Cooking: 4 hrs. Other: soaking the peas 12 hrs. Wine suggestion: not really a wine drinker's dish.

Ingredients   250 g (9 oz) split peas
200 g (7 oz) celeriac or celery
200 g (7 oz) bacon bits
1 pig's tail
3 bayleaves
handful of thyme
handful of sage
1 soupspoon Dijon mustard
1 soupspoon wine vinegar
1⅓ litres (about 2½ pints) water
oil
salt and pepper

Method: Soak the split peas overnight.

Chop the bacon bits. Brush a large pan with oil. Sweat the bacon in oil. Dice the celeriac (or celery) and add to the pan. Add the peas, herbs and water. Chop the pig's tail, wrap the pieces in a muslin cloth and add to the pan. Season. Bring to the boil and simmer 4 hours. Top up with water if necessary. Add the wine vinegar and mustard. Remove the muslin containing the pig's tail. Flake the meat into the soup and discard the bones.

Note: Success with this soup depends on generous use of the herbs. Use a handful of the sage and thyme. One may also make the soup with a little onion and carrot.

Pâtés de Poissons Fumés

Four Smoked Fish Pâtés

Serves: 8. Total cost: 8 units. Preparation: 35–45 mins. Cooking: included in preparation. Wine suggestion: Sylvaner.

Smoked Mackerel Pâté
Ingredients   180g (6–7 oz) smoked mackerel fillets
                    1 tinned tomato
                    1 clove garlic
                    100 ml (3 ½ fl oz) double cream
                    1 soupspoon chopped parsley
                    pepper

Method: Blend all the above ingredients together.

Finnan Haddock Pâté
Ingredients   220 g (8 oz) finnan haddock fillets
                    200 ml (7 fl oz) top of the milk
                    25 g (1 oz) butter
                    1 level teaspoon turmeric
                    3 crushed juniper berries
                    salt and pepper

Method: Poach the haddock in the top of the milk and butter. Add turmeric, juniper berries and seasoning. Blend in the liquidiser.

Kipper Pâté
Ingredients 2 kippers
1 medium onion
2 teaspoons Worcestershire sauce
100 ml (3½ fl oz) double cream
15 g (½ oz) butter

Method: Fry the kippers in a little butter till they are just cooked. Fillet them. Dice the onion. Liquidise the kipper, onion and cream with two teaspoons of Worcestershire sauce.

Smoked Cods' Roe Pâté
Ingredients 120 g (4½ oz) smoked cods' roe
4 slices white bread and a little milk
50 g (scant 2 oz) melted butter
3 cloves garlic
100 ml (3½ fl oz) double cream

Method: Soak the bread without crusts in a little milk. Squeeze out. Liquidise smoked cods' roe, bread, garlic, cream and melted butter.

Note: Though each of these recipes is the essence of simplicity, by combining the separate tastes from the strongest, Smoked Cods' Roe Pâté, to the mildest, Finnan Haddock Pâté, one arrives at an interesting blend of flavour and textures.

The obvious accompaniment is hot toast.

Gougères aux Amandes et au Jambon
'Gougères' with Almonds, Ham and a Madeira Sauce

Serves: 8. Total cost 11 units. Preparation: 15 mins. Cooking: gougères 15 mins, sauce 5 mins. Oven: 204°C/425°F/Gas Mk 7. Wine suggestion: Burgundy – Monthélie.

Ingredients 250 g (9 oz) flour
240 g (8½ oz) butter
150 g (5½ oz) grated cheese (Cheddar, Gruyère, Emmenthal, etc)
7 eggs   *For the sauce:*
500 ml (17 fl oz) water   110 g (4 oz) ham
150 g (5½ oz) almonds   500 ml (17 fl oz) Madeira
salt and cayenne pepper   sauce

Bistro Style Cookery

Method: Make a choux paste from flour, 220 g (8 oz) butter, water, salt, a little cayenne pepper and eggs. Boil water and butter with seasoning. Stir in flour and combine in the pan till the paste comes away easily from the sides.

Transfer the paste to a mixing bowl and beat in the eggs one at a time. Blend the cheese into the choux paste. Melt the rest of the butter. Shake almonds in the butter. Prepare two baking trays with grease-proof paper. Place the gougère mixture in a piping bag with a large plain tube. Pipe eight rings on to the paper. Dispose almonds on the individual rings. Bake in a hot oven about 15 minutes.

Heat the Madeira sauce and add a julienne of ham. Pour a little sauce over each gougère and the rest in a sauce boat.

Main Courses

Ballottine de Caneton au Poivre Vert
Boned and Stuffed Duck with Green Peppercorn Sauce

Serves: 8. Total cost: 24 units. Preparation: duck 45–60 mins, sauce 40–50 mins. Cooking: 90 mins, sauce 30 mins. Oven: 190°C/374°F/Gas Mk 5. Other: marinading the duck 3 hrs, duck stock 3 hrs. Wine suggestion: Burgundy – Gevrey-Chambertin.

Ingredients   1 duck, about 2 kg (4½ lb)
500 g (17–18 oz) chicken leg meat
1 medium onion
2 slices white bread soaked in milk
25 ml (1 fl oz) cognac
50 ml (1¾ fl oz) cream
2 eggs
1 orange
½ lemon
oil
salt and pepper

Method: Turn the duck so the back is uppermost. Remove skin and bones as for a chicken galantine. Set aside skin. (Make a stock with the bones which can be used to make the sauce.) Marinade the duck fillets in cognac. Mince together duck leg meat, liver, heart and chicken legs. Sweat chopped onion in a little oil. Add to farce. Lightly beat eggs. Squeeze the milk from the bread. Grate the orange and lemon zests. Add juice and zests, bread, eggs and seasoning to the meat. Combine with cream.

Spread a layer of farce on the inside of the duck skin. Fill the leg cavities. Cut the fillets into strips. Alternate layers of farce and fillets, finishing with a layer of farce. Fold over the duck skin.

Fasten with cocktail sticks. Mould the ballottine as closely as possible to its original shape. Stick thigh-bones in the stuffed legs. Wrap the ballottine in foil. Bake in a moderate oven for 90 minutes.

Sauce for the Ballottine

Ingredients   1 litre (35 fl oz) duck stock
2 egg whites
1 teaspoon green peppercorns
1 orange
75 ml (scant 3 fl oz) Madeira
1 heaped teaspoon arrowroot
salt

Method: Allow a litre of fresh duck stock to cool. Skim off fat. Lightly beat the whites. Stir the whites into stock. Bring to the boil and simmer for 20 minutes to clarify. Strain. Reduce the clarified stock to about half a litre (17 fl oz). Dissolve the arrowroot in the orange juice. Add to the stock with crushed green peppercorns. Continue simmering till the sauce shines. Season. Add the Madeira off the heat.

Daube à l'Avignonnaise
Lamb Simmered in a Sealed Pot with Orange and Rosemary

Serves: 8. Total cost: 25 units. Preparation: 25–35 mins. Cooking: 4 hrs. Other: 3 hrs marinading the lamb. Oven: 165°C/329°F/Gas Mk 3. Wine suggestion: Côtes du Rhône – Gigondas.

Ingredients
1 boned shoulder of lamb
450 g (1 lb) streaky bacon
4 large onions
2 carrots
4 bayleaves
thyme
zests of 2 oranges
1 litre (1¾ pints) red wine
50 ml (1¾ fl oz) oil
salt and pepper
(flour and water paste)

Method: Slice the shoulder into sixteen pieces, each weighing about 80 g (3 oz). Make an incision in each piece, following the grain. Place a lardon of bacon in each piece. Prepare a marinade with two chopped onions and carrots, bayleaves, thyme, wine, oil, salt and pepper. Arrange the lamb in the marinade and leave for 3 hours, turning from time to time.

Dice the rest of the bacon including the rind. Dice the remaining onions. Put the pieces of lamb in a heavy duty ovenproof dish. Sprinkle with chopped onion, bacon and orange zests. Add the bayleaves from the marinade and a fresh sprig of thyme. Strain the wine from the marinade over the lamb, Bring to the boil. Seal the lid with a flour and water paste. Bake in slow oven for 4 hours.

Note: If one has small individual ovenproof dishes available they are an advantage. One may open them at the table and the customer will benefit from the full bouquet.

Because there is a quantity of fat rendered during the long simmering, something that not all Englishmen relish, one may replace the shoulder with a leg of lamb and use lean instead of streaky bacon.

Cuisses de Volaille aux Epices
Spiced Chicken Legs with Saffron Rice

Serves: 8. Total cost: 18 units. Preparation: 20–30 mins. Cooking: rice 18 mins, chicken 12 mins. Oven: 204°C/425°F/Gas Mk 7. Other: macerating the chicken legs 12 hrs. Wine suggestion: Bordeaux – red Graves or Provence – Bandol.

Ingredients   *For the chicken:*
8 chicken legs
50 ml (1¾ fl oz) oil
2 teaspoons coriander
½ teaspoon cumin
1 teaspoon powdered ginger
½ teaspoon fenugreek
1 pinch dried mustard
1 pinch poppy seed
1 dried chilli
1 teaspoon sea salt
For the rice:
450 g (1 lb) non-stick rice
1 onion
50 g (1¾ oz) butter
2 teaspoons of the above spice mix
850 ml (1½ pints) seasoned chicken stock
2 pinches saffron
For the garnish:
2 pieces stem ginger

Method: Pound or blend in the liquidiser: coriander, cumin, ginger, fenugreek, mustard, poppy seed, chilli and sea salt.

Bone the chicken legs keeping the meat in one piece. Brush with oil. Rub flesh with the spice mixture. Wrap in foil and leave overnight.

Mince the onion. Fry in the butter. Add two teaspoons of the spice mix and the rice. Continue frying for 2 more minutes. Pour over the stock. Cover with a grease-proof lid made from a piece of greaseproof paper cut to cover the pan. Bring to the boil and simmer till the liquid has been absorbed. Stir in the saffron.

Grill the chicken legs skin-side down (next to the heat) for 5 minutes. Transfer to a hot oven and continue cooking for a further 7 minutes.

Finely chop the stem ginger and sprinkle a little over each piece of chicken. Serve on a bed of rice.

Lapin Sauté au Cidre

Sauté of Rabbit with Cider

Serves: 8. Total cost: 18 units. Preparation: 40–50 mins. Cooking: 1½ hrs. Wine suggestion: Rosé de Provence

Ingredients

2 skinned rabbits about
    2½ kg (about 6 lb)
450 g (1 lb) onions
250 g (9 oz) streaky bacon
200 ml (7 fl oz) unprocessed
    olive oil
1 litre (1¾ pints) dry cider

80 g (3 oz) flour
1 lemon
1 soupspoon chopped
    rosemary
salt and pepper
250 g (9 oz) mushrooms
    (optional)

Method: Cut up the rabbits (see fig. 1). Blanch bacon lardons 5 minutes in boiling water. Sauté the rabbit a few pieces at a time in oil, they must be golden. Add bacon and roughly-chopped onions to the pan. Colour. Return rabbit to the pan. Sprinkle with flour. Add cider, rosemary and seasoning. Simmer till tender, about 1½ hours depending on whether the rabbit was wild or not. It will be longer if it was. Add the mushrooms and lemon juice. Serve with croûtons fried in olive oil.

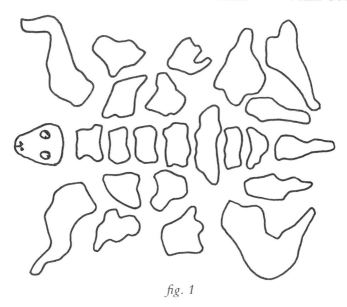

fig. 1

Pot-au-Feu

French Boiled Beef

Serves: 8. Total cost: 32 units. Preparation: 40–50 mins. Cooking: 3½ hrs. Wine suggestion: Bordeaux – St Emilion.

Ingredients   2 kg (4½ lb) shin of beef
2 marrow bones sawn into pieces
6 medium carrots
6 leeks
2 sticks celery
2 large onions, each piqué with two cloves
2 cloves garlic
bouquet garni
25 g (scant 1 oz) Dijon mustard
salt and pepper
For the vegetables:
1 head celery
1 kg (2¼ lb) carrots
1 kg (2¼ lb) potatoes
1 kg (2¼ lb) leeks
1 kg (2¼ lb) young turnips

Method: Bring a gallon of water to the boil (or half stock, half water) with the first batch of vegetables, bouquet garni and salt. Add the shin and bones. Simmer for 3½ hours. Skim off any impurities that rise to the surface during cooking.

Prepare the vegetables. Cut the celery into 5 cm (2 in) pieces. Tie with string or place in muslin bags. Similarly with carrots and leeks. Peel turnips and potatoes.

After 2¾ hours simmering add the carrots to the pot-au-feu. After 3 hours the remaining vegetables and garlic.

Remove meat, tied vegetables, potatoes and turnips. Strain the liquid into a fresh saucepan. Whisk in mustard. Check seasoning. Arrange the meat and vegetables on a serving dish. Serve the stock separately in soup tureens.

Accompany with Dijon mustard and gherkins.

Note: One can imagine plenty of chefs thinking that pot-au-feu is impractical as a restaurant dish. Once it has been prepared, the meat may be kept hot in half of the cooking liquid. The vegetables may be re-heated to order in the rest of the liquid or some consommé.

Hochepot de Queue de Boeuf

Oxtail Hot-pot

Serves: 8. Total cost: 19 units. Preparation: 25–35 mins. Cooking: 3 hrs. Other: Soaking oxtails 2 hrs. Wine suggestion: Côtes du Rhône Villages.

Ingredients
2 oxtails
3 large carrots
3 large onions
650 g (23 oz) young turnips
250 g (9 oz) cooked haricots blancs or butter beans
200 ml (7 fl oz) red wine
1½ litres (about 2½ pints) consommé
30 g (1 oz) tomato purée
90 g (3 oz) flour
oil
salt and pepper
(1 lettuce)

Method: Soak the oxtails in cold water for 2 hours. Colour the oxtail a few pieces at a time in a large pan and reserve. Just brush the bottom of the pan with oil; one should not need fat. Stir in the flour. Make a brown roux. Add diced onion and carrot. Mix in tomato purée. Return pieces of oxtail to the pan. Pour over stock and then wine. Season. Cover and simmer for 2 hours.

Add chopped turnips (small purple ones if you can obtain them). Continue simmering for a further hour until the meat is almost falling off the bone. 10 minutes before serving add the cooked haricots blancs.

Note: Oxtail renders a good deal of fat during cooking. A few lettuce leaves in the sauce absorb excess fat like blotting paper. The beans and turnips also absorb fat.

Goujonettes de Barbue Choron
Strips of Brill Fried with Tomato and Hollandaise Sauce

Serves: 8. Total cost: 16 units. Preparation: 20–25 mins. Cooking: 5 mins. Wine suggestion: Loire – Sancerre.

Ingredients   1 kg (2¼ lb) brill fillets
flour
egg-wash
breadcrumbs
1 clove garlic
200 ml (7 fl oz) olive oil
salt and pepper
For the sauce:
300 ml (10½ fl oz) Hollandaise sauce
1 tomato
2 cloves garlic
1 soupspoon tomato purée
tarragon
salt and pepper

Method: Skin the fillets and cut them into strips about 5 cm (2 in) by 1½ cm (½ in). Coat them in the flour, egg-wash and breadcrumbs. Rub the pan with garlic. Add the olive oil and heat. Fry the goujonettes a few pieces at a time. Sprinkle with salt as you remove them from the pan.

For the sauce, crush the garlic with salt. Beat it into the Hollandaise. Stir in the tomato purée. Blanch, skin and pip the tomato. Dice it finely and add to the sauce. Check seasoning. Finish with chopped fresh tarragon.

Note: If you cannot get tarragon (difficult to find in winter) use parsley.

Quenelles de Poisson aux Coquilles St Jacques

Fish Quenelles with a Scallop and Cream Sauce

Serves: 8. Total cost: 21 units. Preparation: 10–15 mins plus quenelles mixture. Cooking: quenelles 10 mins, sauce 10 mins. Other: chilling quenelles 1 hr. Wine suggestion: Chablis.

Ingredients
1 batch of fish quenelle mixture (see page 35)
200 ml (7 fl oz) fumet
200 ml (7 fl oz) white wine
200 ml (7 fl oz) double cream
12 scallops
1 teaspoon chopped parsley
pepper

Method: Reduce the white wine with 200 ml (7 fl oz) of the fumet used for poaching the quenelles. Add the cream and continue reduction. Just before the sauce has reached coating consistency, add the corals from the scallops and a little white pepper. If the fumet was well seasoned the sauce should not need salt. Slice the scallop meat (about three pieces per scallop). Toss them into the boiling sauce. Stir in parsley and remove from heat.

Drain the poached quenelles (two per person) and coat with the sauce. The commonest fault is to overcook the scallops, so do not add them to the reduction until the sauce is ready to be served. You can 'relever' the sauce with a little Hollandaise whisked in just after adding the scallops.

Suprême de Volaille en Papillote

Stuffed Breast of Chicken

Serves: 8. Total cost: 18 units: Preparation: 50–60 mins. Cooking: 20 mins. Other: chilling forcemeat 1 hr. Oven: 235°C/455°F/Gas Mk 8. Wine suggestion: Burgundy – Puligny Montrachet.

Ingredients   8 chicken breasts with winglets attached
100 g (3½ oz) butter
oil
salt and pepper
For the farce:
1 boned chicken leg
1 slice stale white bread
1 large egg white
75 ml (2½ fl oz) double cream
1 pinch mace or 1 pinch allspice
salt and pepper
(milk)
For the sauce:
300 ml (10 fl oz) Hollandaise sauce
100 ml (3½ fl oz) cream
1 large pinch mace

Method: Remove the fillets from the chicken breasts. Brush them with oil and tap them out lightly with a cutlet bat, between two sheets of greaseproof paper. Set aside. Using the point of a sharp knife, cut along the thick side of the breasts to make pockets for the stuffing.

Blend the chicken leg to a purée in the liquidiser. Season with salt, pepper, allspice or mace. Soak the bread (without crust) in milk. Squeeze out as much moisture as possible. Add to the leg and blend well. Repeat the process with the egg white. Place in the fridge for 1 hour. Add the cream (from the fridge, too) to the purée. Blend to a smooth paste.

Spread some farce in each pocket of breast. Spread the remainder on top. Cover the top layer of farce with the flattened fillets. Season. Wrap each breast in buttered greaseproof paper. Bake in a hot oven 20 minutes.

Pour the butter and juice from each breast into the Hollandaise. Whisk well. Add the mace. Beat the cream till quite stiff. Fold into sauce. Coat the chicken with a little sauce and serve the remainder separately in a sauce boat.

Sweets

Granité aux Mandarines

Mandarin Water-ice

Serves: 8. Total cost: 4 units. Preparation: 15 mins. Cooking: none. Other: freezing.

Ingredients   10 mandarin oranges
200 g (7 oz) sugar
1 lemon
50 ml (1 ¾ fl oz) Cointreau

Method: Wash the mandarins under the tap to remove chemicals in the zests. Peel the zests. Place in a pan with sugar and 150 ml (5 fl oz) water. Boil. Reduce to a syrup.

Blend the mandarins in a liquidiser. Add 150 ml (5 fl oz) cold water. Combine the strained syrup, liquidised mandarins and the juice of a lemon.

Place in the freezer till almost set, but not solid. Beat the mixture. One will obtain a crushed-ice rather than a sorbet texture. Spoon the granité into glass coupes. Pour a dash of Cointreau over each one and serve immediately.

Note: A granité is an alternative to a sorbet, useful for those who do not have ice-cream making machines. However, if you leave it too long in the freezer it will set like an outsize lollipop. So temperatures need watching.

Tarte aux Pommes Caramelisées

Caramelised Apple Tart

Serves: 8. Total cost: 5 units. Preparation: 20–30 mins. Cooking: 20 mins. Oven: 235°C/455°F/Gas Mk 8.

Ingredients   200 g (7 oz) lump or granulated sugar
1 kg (2¼ lb) eating apples
350 g (12–13 oz) feuilletage (see page 42)
1 egg white
1 coffeespoon cinnamon
1 coffeespoon powdered ginger

Method: Place the sugar in a large metal flan ring or baking tray. Moisten with water. Place over a flame and heat to a dark amber caramel. Work the caramel while still hot over the bottom and sides of the flan ring.

Peel and finely slice the apples. Sprinkle with powdered cinnamon and ginger. Arrange in closely overlapping layers on the caramel. Roll out the feuilletage, brush with lightly beaten egg white and place egg white side down on the apple. Bake in a very hot oven for up to 20 minutes (till the puff pastry has set).

Remove from the oven. Allow to cool slightly. Turn out on to a large dish.

Poires Glacées au Vin Rouge
Pears Glazed in Red Wine

Serves: 8. Total cost: 9 units. Preparation: 20–25 mins. Cooking: 40–60 mins. Other: to chill the pears 4 hrs.

Ingredients
8 pears
1 bottle of red wine
300 g (11–12 oz) sugar
1 lemon
1 coffeespoon cinnamon
1 coffeespoon nutmeg

Method: Put the wine in a stainless steel saucepan with lemon slices, sugar and spices. Bring to the boil. Peel the pears leaving the stalks in place. Drop them in the boiling syrup to poach. Cover the pan. Simmer gently for 40 to 60 minutes. Baste any uncovered parts of the pears during this time.

Drain the pears and place them on a dish. Remove the slices of lemon from the syrup. Reduce the sugar and wine rapidly till it reaches a coating consistency. Coat the pears with the syrup. Chill.

Note: Serve with crème Chantilly to which a little pear eau-de-vie has been added.

Brown Bread Ice-cream

Serves: 8. Total cost: 8 units. Preparation: 20–30 mins. Cooking: none. Other: drying bread 25 mins, to freeze the ice-cream 6 hrs.

Ingredients 3 thick slices of stale wholemeal bread
8 yolks
220 g (8 oz) castor sugar
900 ml (1 ½ pints) double cream
vanilla essence

Method: Beat together the yolks and castor sugar till the mixture has whitened and stiffened. It is ready when it folds like a ribbon when poured off the spatula.

Add a few drops of vanilla essence to the cream. Whip till it is stiff enough to hold its shape on the whisk.

Place the brown bread in a warm oven to dry out. This will take about 25 minutes. Be careful not to let the toast brown. When crisp crush between two pieces of foil with a rolling pin.

Combine yolk mixture with cream. Fold in the brown breadcrumbs. Place in the freezer until the ice-cream is on the point of setting. Remove and beat again. This increases the volume and breaks down any remaining crystals. Return to the freezer and allow to set.

Note: Raspberry purée to accompany the ice-cream. Stew 250 g (9 oz) frozen raspberries with sugar to taste. Blend them in the liquidiser. Strain through a fine sieve.

Galette des Rois
Twelfth Night Pastry

Serves: 8. Total cost: 11 units. Preparation: 45–50 mins. Cooking: 25 mins. Oven: 235°C/455°F/Gas Mk 7.

Ingredients 750 g (27 oz) feuilletage (page 42)
1 large yolk
For the almond cream:
80 g (3 oz) ground almonds
80 g (3 oz) unsalted butter
80 g (3 oz) castor sugar
1 soupspoon cornflour
1 egg
1 soupspoon rum
For the crème pâtissière:
75 ml (2 ½ fl oz) milk
1 yolk
1 heaped teaspoon cornflour
20 g (¾ oz) castor sugar

Method: Make the crème pâtissière: beat yolk, cornflour and sugar. Pour over hot milk to dissolve. Place mixture in a fresh pan. Bring to the boil. Stir till thickened. Cool.

Beat together almonds, butter, sugar, cornflour, egg and rum. Combine with crème pâtissière. Place in a fresh pan. Bring to the boil stirring throughout.

Divide the feuilletage into two equal parts. Roll out into two circles, about ½ cm (¼ in) thick. Place one circle on buttered greaseproof paper, on a baking tray. Brush the edge with water. Spread the crème on top. Spread the second circle on top of that. Seal the edges. Glaze the top ring with egg yolk. Decorate with the point of a sharp knife. Bake 25 minutes in a very hot oven.

Note: Because this is a very simple recipe, traditionally served on Twelfth Night (La Fête des Rois), the success depends on excellent pastry which must be both light and fresh. Make it as close to the time it will be eaten as possible.

Fig. 1   (Decoration of pastry)

Négus
Bitter Chocolate and Coffee Gâteau

Serves: 8. Total cost: 11 units. Preparation: 50–60 mins. Cooking: 30–40 mins. Other: setting the filling 2 hrs. Oven: 190°C/374°F/Gas Mk 5.

Ingredients   *For the génoise:*
8 standard eggs (or 6 duck eggs)
300 g (11 oz) castor sugar
120 g (4½ oz) flour
80 g (3 oz) unsweetened cocoa
flour and butter for the cake tin(s)
For the filling:
8 standard eggs
400 g (14 oz) castor sugar
300 g (11 oz) bitter chocolate
a small cup of very strong black coffee
120 g (4½ oz) unsalted butter
For the garnish:
chocolate vermicelli

Method: Work the yolks and sugar till they have whitened. Rain the flour and cocoa into the mixture. Mix in well. Beat the whites to stiff peaks. Fold them into the cocoa mixture. Pour into a large, steep-sided génoise tin previously floured and buttered. Transfer immediately to a moderate oven. Bake for 30 to 40 minutes.

To make the filling, place the eggs and sugar in an enamel or copper pan. Whisk over a gentle heat until the mixture becomes the consistency of a thinned Hollandaise (just before the eggs start to scramble). Melt chocolate with the butter and coffee in a bain-marie. Combine the chocolate and egg mixtures. Place in the fridge and leave for about 2 hours to set.

When the génoise has cooled, slice it into three discs. Spread a layer of filling on each disc, the top and sides of the gâteau. Sprinkle with chocolate vermicelli to cover.

Note: Success of this recipe depends on using a really good cocoa powder which gives a dark colour and slightly bitter taste to the gâteau. Otherwise it can taste very much like an ordinary chocolate cake.

Menu 2
February–March

First Courses

Main Courses

Sweets

First Courses

Terrine de Saumon Fumé
Smoked Salmon Terrine

Serves: 8. Total cost: 13 units. Preparation: 40–50 mins. Cooking: none. Other: to set the terrine 2 hrs. Wine suggestion: Riesling.

Ingredients
220 g (8 oz) smoked salmon
2 yolks
1 teaspoon Dijon mustard
1 teaspoon tomato purée
1 lemon
175 ml (6 fl oz) groundnut oil
125 ml (4 ½ fl oz) double cream
4 leaves of gelatine
salt and pepper

Method: Place a small terrine in the freezer.

Soak the gelatine in cold water.

Liquidise 150 g (5 oz) smoked salmon with a little cream.

Prepare a mayonnaise with yolks, lemon juice, mustard, tomato purée, oil, salt and a generous quantity of milled pepper. Combine the purée of salmon with the mayonnaise. Whip the cream till stiff. Fold into the mixture. Dissolve the gelatine.

Take the terrine from the freezer. Dip the rest of the smoked salmon, cut into extra fine slices, into the gelatine. Line the terrine with these pieces. Stir the remaining gelatine into the prepared mixture. Fill the terrine. Place in the fridge to set. Turn out.

Moules aux Coquilles
Scallops with Mussels

Serves: 8. Total cost: 16 units. Preparation: 10–15 mins. Cooking: mussels 10 mins, sauce 10 mins. Other: cleaning mussels 20 mins. Wine suggestion: Muscadet.

Ingredients
40 mussels
8 large scallops
1 onion
300 ml (10 fl oz) white wine
30 g (1 oz) butter

200 ml (7 fl oz) double cream
15 g (½ oz) celery leaves
saffron
pepper

Method: Dice the onion as finely as possible. Soften in the butter without colouring. Dice the celery leaves. Add to the pan. Pour over the wine. Place the scrubbed mussels in the pan. Bring to the boil. Cover and simmer till the mussels have opened.

Strain the cooking liquid into a fresh pan. Reduce by two-thirds. Add the cream and continue the reduction. When almost at a coating consistency, add the scallops. Simmer for 3 minutes. Season with pepper and enough saffron to turn the sauce a pale yellow.

Arrange the mussels in half their shells on individual serving dishes. Place the scallop in the middle. Coat with sauce.

Note: It is unlikely that any salt will be needed to season this recipe.

There is a tendency to overcook scallops. If they are fresh you should leave them in the pan only long enough to heat through. Frozen scallops lose their liquid in freezing. They also toughen much more quickly than fresh ones.

Navets au Jambon
Baby Turnips Baked with Ham

Serves: 8. Total cost: 10 units. Preparation: 15–20 mins. Cooking: turnips 15 mins, sauce 15 mins, baking 20 mins. Oven: 200°C/392°F/Gas Mk 6. Wine suggestion: Sylvaner.

Ingredients   16 small turnips
                     200 g (7 oz) Gruyère
                     200 g (7 oz) ham
                     salt
                     For the sauce:
                     30 g (1 oz) butter
                     30 g (1 oz) flour
                     500 ml (17 fl oz) milk
                     1 soupspoon kirsch
                     110 g (4 oz) grated Gruyère
                     nutmeg
                     salt and pepper

Method: Blanch the turnips in boiling, salted water for 15 minutes. Prepare a béchamel sauce. Melt the butter. Add the flour. Pour in the milk a third at a time. Bring to the boil. Reduce by a half. Add the grated Gruyère, kirsch, nutmeg, salt and pepper. Simmer 5 minutes more.

Slice each turnip into three. Place a slice of ham and a slice of Gruyère in each turnip. Reconstitute.

Put the turnips in an ovenproof dish. Coat with the cheese sauce. Bake in a hottish oven for 20 minutes.

Tourrin Bordelais
Onion and Tomato Soup

Serves: 8. Total cost: 8 units. Preparation: 20–25 mins. Cooking: 60 mins. Wine suggestion: not really necessary to drink a separate wine with this. Choose in accordance with main course.

Ingredients	4 onions
	1 carrot
	1 branch celery
	450 g (1 lb) tomatoes
	50 g (scant 2 oz) beef dripping
	2¼ litres (4 pints) consommé
	thyme
	bayleaf
	4 yolks
	salt and pepper

Method: Blanch and peel the tomatoes and blend them in the liquidiser. Finely dice carrot and celery. Heat the dripping. Sweat the carrot and celery in the fat. Slice the onions. Add them to the pan. Pour over the tomatoes and consommé. Add the thyme and bayleaf. Bring to the boil and simmer for an hour. Check the seasoning. Whisk the soup on to the yolks a little at a time.

Terrine de Lapin à la Bénédictine
Terrine of Rabbit with Bénédictine

Serves: 10. Total cost: 7 units. Preparation: 20–30 mins. Cooking: 2 hrs plus 1¼ hrs. Other: marinading 12 hrs, resting 24 hrs. Oven: 190°C/374°F/Gas Mk 5. Wine suggestion: Gamay de Tours.

Ingredients   400 g (14 oz) rabbit meat
200 g (7 oz) lean pork
200 g (7 oz) fat bacon
1 rabbit liver
1 rabbit head and carcass
1 large onion
3 cloves garlic
100 ml (3 ½ fl oz) white wine
75 ml (2 ½ fl oz) Bénédictine
3 juniper berries
2 bayleaves
salt and pepper
(flour and water paste)

Method: Place the rabbit head and carcass in a pan with three pints of water and half the white wine. Add one bayleaf, the onion and a few peppercorns. Bring to the boil. Skim. Reduce slowly, about 2 hours, until less than a cup of glaze remains.

Dice half the rabbit meat. Mince the rest, including the liver, with pork and bacon, keeping back two slices of bacon for the terrine. Crush the garlic, juniper berries and the other bayleaf. Prepare a marinade with the remainder of the wine, half the Bénédictine and the spices. Season heavily with pepper. Combine the meats. Place in the marinade. Mix in the glaze before it sets. Leave overnight.

Line the bottom of a terrine with two slices of bacon. Add a little salt to the pâté mixture. Fill the terrine.

Prepare a flour and water paste, stiff enough to resemble putty. Seal the lid of the terrine with the paste by putting a strip round its rim and fixing the lid on top. Place in a bain-marie and bake in a moderate oven for about 1¼ hours.

Remove the terrine. Allow to cool for 1 hour. Remove lid. Pour rest of the Bénédictine over the pâté. Weight the pâté with a minimum of one kilogram. Leave 24 hours before serving.

Beignets Soufflés au Coulis de Tomates
Cheese and Choux Pastry Deep-fried with Tomato

Serves: 8. Total cost: 5 units. Preparation: 20–25 mins. Cooking: beignets 5 mins, coulis 20 mins. Oil temperature: 180°C/356°F. Wine suggestion: Sauvignon.

Ingredients   150 g (5 ½ oz) flour
300 ml (10 fl oz) water
100 g (3 ½ oz) butter
100 g (3 ½ oz) Gruyère
4 eggs
salt and pepper
For the coulis:
450 g (1 lb) tinned tomatoes
1 onion
2 cloves garlic
thyme
oregano
40 g (1 ½ oz) butter
salt and pepper
deep frying oil

Method: Dice onion and garlic. Sweat in butter till golden. Add the tomatoes, a large sprig of thyme and a pinch of oregano. Simmer 20 minutes. Check the seasoning.

Make a choux paste. Place butter and water in a pan. Bring to the boil. When the mixture bubbles up the sides of the pan, rain in the flour. Beat until the flour is incorporated. Transfer the paste to a mixing bowl. Cool 5 minutes. Beat in the eggs one at a time till the mixture shines. Mix in the grated Gruyère.

Heat a pan of frying oil. Use two spoons to shape the beignet mix into little nuggets. Drop into the oil. Fry for 5 minutes. Drain on kitchen paper. Sprinkle with a little salt. Serve on a bed of tomato.

Soupe de Congre au Safran

Conger Eel Soup with Herbs and Saffron

Serves: 8. Total cost: 11 units. Preparation: 15–20 mins. Cooking: 30 mins. Wine suggestion: Beaujolais blanc.

Ingredients   8 conger eel steaks taken from the head and tied like noisettes of lamb
2 lettuces
2 soupspoons chopped parsley
3 lemons (or 2 lemons and 15 g (½ oz) sorrel)
2 onions
1 g (a sachet) saffron
2 cloves garlic
500 ml (17 fl oz) fumet
1 ½ litres (2¼ pints) water
100 ml (3 ½ fl oz) cream
2 yolks
salt and pepper
100 ml (3 ½ fl oz) olive oil
8 slices French bread

Method: Chop the lettuce. Dice the onion and garlic. Place lettuce, onion, garlic and parsley in a pan. Arrange the conger on top. Moisten with lemon juice, fumet and water. Bring to the boil and season. Simmer for 30 to 40 minutes according to the eels' quality.

Fry the bread in oil. Arrange on hot soup plates. Cut the string tying the pieces of eels. Place on the croûtons. Mix the yolks and cream together. Whisk into the soup off the heat. Add saffron. Serve the soup from a tureen.

Main Courses

Falette

Breast of Veal Filled with Pâté and Braised in Wine ·

Serves: 8. Total cost: 25 units. Preparation: 45–60 mins. Cooking: 2–2½ hr. Oven: 165°C/353°F/Gas Mk 4. Wine: Bordeaux – Margaux.

Ingredients   piece of veal 30 cm (12 in) by 26 cm (10 in) cut
lengthwise from the breast of veal trimmed of bones
200 g (7 oz) minced veal
200 g (7 oz) minced belly of pork
200 g (7 oz) lean bacon
2 medium onions
3 cloves garlic
30 g (1 oz) chopped parsley
1 egg
salt and pepper
For the braising stock:
150 g (5½ oz) streaky bacon
3 carrots
3 onions
250 ml (7 fl oz) veal stock
250 ml (7 fl oz) white wine
parsley stalks
rosemary
salt and pepper

Method: Using a carving knife make a slit through the middle of the veal, along its longer side to form a sleeve. Prepare a farce with minced veal, pork, bacon, onions, garlic, parsley, egg and seasoning. Stuff the sleeve of veal. Sow up the extremities.

Sweat the bacon in a pan large enough to take the piece of veal. Slice the carrot and onion. Add them to the pan. When they begin to colour, place the veal on top. Colour the veal on all sides. It must be golden all over. Pour over the veal stock and wine. Add the parsley stalks, a large sprig of rosemary, salt and pepper. Bring liquid to boil. Cover pan. Braise in a moderate oven for 2 to 2½ hours.

Fig. 1   Cross section of Falette. The farce is in the dark area.

Note: As an accompaniment to Falette prepare two lettuces and three heads of chicory. Make a dressing with five soupspoons walnut oil, juice of half a lemon, salt and pepper. Toss the lettuce and chicory in the dressing. Garnish with 50 g (scant 2 oz) walnuts.

Aillade de Mouton

Hogget with Garlic, Tomato and Parsley

Serves: 8. Total cost: 17 units. Preparation: 20–30 mins. Cooking: 1½–2 hrs. Wine suggestion: Bandol.

Ingredients
1 boned shoulder hogget (or mutton)
10 large cloves garlic
700 g (about 1 ½ lb) tinned tomatoes
5 shallots
1 soupspoon chopped parsley
1 hcaped soupspoon chopped fresh rosemary
1 heaped soupspoon thyme
100 ml (3 ½ fl oz) white wine
100 ml (3 ½ fl oz) olive oil
salt and pepper

Method: Cube the meat into domino sized pieces. Fry till the meat is well coloured on all sides. Deglaze the pan with the wine. Crush the garlic. Dice the shallots. Add the tomatoes, shallots and herbs to the pan. Season. Cover. Simmer gently for 1 ½ to 2 hours, depending on the quality of the meat. Garnish with chopped parsley.

Poulet Sauté au Chinon

Chicken Sauté with Chinon Wine

Serves: 8. Total cost: 29 units. Preparation: 25–35 mins. Cooking: sauce 1 hr, chicken 12 mins. Wine suggestion: Chinon.

Ingredients
2 chickens
600 g (21 oz) streaky bacon
600 g (21 oz) button mushrooms
80 g (3 oz) shallots
1 clove garlic
700 ml (1¼ pints) chicken stock
700 ml (1 bottle) Chinon
25 ml (1 fl oz) groundnut oil
1 heaped teaspoon arrowroot
salt and pepper
For the garnish:
1 heaped teaspoon chopped parsley
1 level teaspoon fresh thyme

Method: Bone the chickens (see Poulet à l'Etuvée, page 25). Keep carcass for stock. Combine stock with the wine. Bring to the boil. Start reducing. Chop the piece of bacon into lardons. Blanch in the reducing liquid for 10 minutes and drain. Fry till they are well coloured in the groundnut oil. Drain. Retain the fat for frying the pieces of chicken.

Quarter the mushrooms if they are on the large side. Poach them in the liquid 10 minutes. Set aside.

When the liquid has reduced by about two-thirds, thicken it with arrowroot. Sauté the pieces of chicken a few pieces at a time (see Poulet Sauté Chasseur, page 30). Set aside. Chop shallots and clove of garlic. Deglaze pan with the sauce. Add the shallots and garlic. Add the mushrooms and lardons to the pan. Simmer 10 minutes. Take off the heat. Return the chicken pieces to the pan. Season. Allow to stand 5 minutes. Serve garnished with parsley and thyme.

Note: It is almost impossible to do Coq au Vin in this country because there are no cocks. Rather than casserole the chicken which is intended for roasting or sautéing, this method gives a better-textured, better-flavoured end product.

One may replace Chinon by a Gamay de Tours, a Beaujolais or any good quality V.D.Q.S. wine. The dish changes its name accordingly.

Cervelles de Veaux aux Lentilles
Spiced Calves' Brains with Lentils and Chorizo

Serves: 8. Total cost: 15 units. Preparation: 40–50 mins. Cooking: brains 15 mins, lentils 1 hr. Other: soaking brains 2 hrs 20 mins. Wine suggestion: V.D.Q.S. Roussillon.

Ingredients   4 sets calves' brains
500 g (18 oz) brown lentils
250 g (9 oz) chorizo sausage
2 cloves garlic
75 ml (2½ fl oz) olive oil
1 large onion
1 medium tin tomatoes
25 ml (1 fl oz) vinegar
30 g (1 oz) flour
30 g (1 oz) paprika
cayenne pepper
salt and pepper

Method: Soak the brains 20 minutes in half the vinegar and warm water. Carefully remove blood and membrane. Transfer to cold water and add the rest of the vinegar. Soak for 2 hours. Place the sets in a pan of salted water. Bring to the boil and poach for 15 minutes.

Place the lentils in a pan. Cover with water and 25 ml (1 fl oz) of oil. Simmer for 30 minutes. Meanwhile, slice the onion, mince the garlic and colour them in a little oil. Add sliced chorizo, tomatoes and cayenne pepper to taste. Drain the lentils and add them to the sauce. Simmer for 1 hour.

Cut the brains into medaillons. Dust with seasoned flour and paprika. Sauté in hot oil. Serve on a bed of lentils.

Raie à la Sauce Bâtarde
Skate with a Butter and Lemon Sauce

Serves: 8. Total cost: 18 units. Preparation: 15–20 mins. Cooking: fish 10–15 mins, sauce 15 mins. Wine suggestion: Loire–Sancerre.

Ingredients 8 × 250 g (9 oz) wings of skate
200 ml (7 fl oz) vinegar
water
salt
For the sauce:
40 g (1 ½ oz) butter
40 g (1 ½ oz) flour
1 ½ lemons
50 ml (1 ¾ fl oz) cream
2 yolks
80 g (3 oz) unsalted butter
salt and pepper

Method: Pour the vinegar into a large pan of salted water. Poach skate for 10 to 15 minutes. Drain and skin.

Make a blond roux with flour and butter. Pour 400 ml (14 fl oz) boiling water and a little of the poaching liquor over the roux. Cook 15 minutes. Season. Mix yolks, cream and lemon juice. Whisk the sauce a little at a time on to the liaison. Whisk in the softened, unsalted butter (or blend in liquidiser); chop the butter into small pieces beforehand. Pour the sauce over the skate.

Note: According to the *Larousse Gastronomique*, skate is different from other fish in that it is better two or three days after being caught, though this does not mean that it should be served high.

Coquilles Provençale
Scallops with Tomato, Onion, Garlic and Herbs

Serves: 8. Total cost: 32 units. Preparation: 25–30 mins. Cooking: 4–5 mins. Wine suggestion: Muscadet.

Ingredients
32 scallops
100 ml (3 ½ fl oz) olive oil
80 g (3 oz) white breadcrumbs
3 cloves garlic
2 soupspoons chopped parsley
salt and pepper
For the tomato mixture:
1 kg (2¼ lb) tomatoes
450 g (1 lb) onions
2 cloves garlic
1 heaped teaspoon Herbes de Provence
  (or fresh basil if available)
1 teaspoon brown sugar
50 ml (1¾ fl oz) olive oil
salt and pepper

Method: Finely dice the onion. Sweat in the olive oil without colouring. Skin the tomatoes (12 seconds in boiling water if they are very ripe). Chop the tomatoes. Add them to the onions with 2 cloves crushed garlic, Herbes de Provence, sugar and seasoning. Allow to stew gently till the tomatoes form a 'coulis' – a rich purée.

When they are ready, heat the oil for the scallops. Crush the 3 cloves of garlic. Add garlic and scallops to the pan with the oil. Sprinkle seasoned crumbs over the scallops. Sauté rapidly for 2 or 3 minutes shaking the pan vigorously; the crumbs will stick to the scallops and colour. Arrange the scallops on a bed of tomatoes. Garnish with chopped parsley.

Note: One will not find fresh basil at this time of year. Basil would be ideal for this dish. The best way to have basil the whole year round is to preserve it in olive oil. Press the leaves tightly in a jar. Cover with olive oil.

Carbonnade Flamande
Beef Braised with Beer and Onions

Serves: 8. Total cost: 15 units. Preparation: 25–30 mins. Cooking: 2 hrs. Oven: 180°C/356°F/Gas Mk 4. Wine suggestion: Burgundy – Côte de Nuits.

Ingredients   1400 g (about 50 oz) skirt
4 onions
1 litre (1¾ pints) brown ale
60 g (2 oz) dripping
60 g (2 oz) flour
1 level soupspoon soft brown sugar
30 g (1 oz) plain chocolate
salt and pepper

Method: Slice the pieces of skirt on the slant. Allow two pieces per portion. Heat the dripping till it is almost smoking. Fry the meat in this fat. Sprinkle with the brown sugar. Drain the pieces of meat.

Slice the onions and fry them in the same fat. Return the beef to the pan. Add the flour and allow to cook for 5 minutes. Pour over the brown ale. Season. Cover. Bake in the oven for 1 hour.

Remove from the oven, add the chocolate. Once it has melted, re-cover the pan and return to the oven for a further hour's cooking.

Note: When frying meat there is a temptation to take it out of the pan before it has coloured properly. 'Well coloured' means that each side of the meat has a dark russet or brown crust. One of the tricks in glossy cookery books is to photograph the meat at this stage glazed with caramelised sugar.

Lapin à la Roquebrussanne
Rabbit with Forcemeat Balls Baked in Wine

Serves: 8. Total cost: 25 units. Preparation: 45–60 mins. Cooking: 1 hr 50 mins. Oven: 154°C/335°F/Gas Mk 3. Wine suggestion: Burgundy – Santenay.

Ingredients   2 small rabbits
200 g (7 oz) minced veal
200 g (7 oz) gammon
2 eggs
300 g (11 oz) onions
2 cloves garlic
1 litre (1¾ pints) white wine
2 soupspoons cognac
150 ml (5 fl oz) olive oil
a large bouquet garni of fennel, celery leaves, rosemary,
    thyme, parsley and bayleaf
1 soupspoon each of parsley, rosemary and thyme
8 skinned tomatoes
salt and pepper

Method: Colour the jointed rabbits in olive oil. Place in a large ovenproof dish with wine, bouquet garni and seasoning. Cover and place in a warm oven to simmer gently.

Mince the gammon, onion and garlic. Blend with the minced veal. Season with chopped herbs. Pepper, but do not salt. Lightly beat the eggs. Bind the forcemeat with egg. Moisten with cognac (marc or any eau-de-vie). Roll the stuffing into small dumplings.

After 1 hour's simmering add the forcemeat balls to the rabbit. Simmer a further ½ hour then add the whole tomatoes. Let them stew for 20 minutes more. Serve.

Note: One may replace the white wine by a Rosé de Provence. Choose tomatoes that are 'sweet', since acidy ones will spoil the flavour of the wine and herbs.

Alouette sans Tête

Beef Paupiettes in Madeira Sauce

Serves: 8. Total cost: 34 units. Preparation: 30–40 mins. Cooking: 20 mins. Oven: 235°C/455°F/Gas Mk 8. Wine suggestion: Bordeaux – St. Estèphe.

Ingredients   8 × 100 g (3 ½ oz) lean sirloin steaks
50 g (scant 2 oz) butter
salt and pepper
For the farce:
2 oranges
140 g (5 oz) onions
1 soupspoon chopped parsley
110 g (4 oz) white breadcrumbs
1 teaspoon chopped rosemary
1 egg
30 g (1 oz) butter
salt and pepper
500 ml (17 ½ fl oz) Madeira sauce (see page 41)

Method: Tap out the steaks with a cutlet bat till they are thin enough for paupiettes. Finely chop the onion. Sweat in the butter. Add the grated zest of the oranges, a little juice, the parsley, crumbs, chopped rosemary and lightly beaten egg. Season. Spread a little of the farce on to each piece of meat. Roll up like a cigarette tucking in the flaps at both ends.

Butter eight pieces of foil. Season the alouettes. Wrap them in foil. Bake in a hot oven for 20 minutes. Remove from their foil. Coat with Madeira sauce.

Entrecôte à la Parilla

Entrecôte Steaks with Chilli and Garlic Dressing

Serves: 8. Total cost: 30 units. Preparation: 10 mins. Cooking: 7–14 mins. Other: Boning the sirloin. Wine suggestion: Rioja – Marquis de Riscal.

Ingredients   8 × 200 g (7 oz) sirloin steaks
grilling oil
salt and pepper
For the parilla:
3 small onions
2 cloves garlic
1 soupspoon parsley
3 soupspoons red wine vinegar
juice of a lemon
1 chilli
salt and pepper

Method: Mince the onion and garlic. Combine with parsley, vinegar, lemon juice, finely diced chilli and seasoning. Place in a small pan and heat gently. Do not allow to cook. Brush the steaks with grilling oil (See page 32). Grill to order. Season. Spoon a little of the parilla over each steak.

Note: The flavour of onion and chilli will develop overnight if the Parilla is used two days running. It should be prepared fresh every day rather than prepared in large quantities.

Sweets

Soufflé au Chocolat
Hot Chocolate Soufflé

Serves: 8. Total cost: 10 units. Preparation: 20 mins. Cooking: about 10 mins. Other: cooling the chocolate 45 mins. Oven: 204°C/425°F/Gas Mk 7.

Ingredients　500 g (18 oz) plain chocolate　50 g (2 oz) butter
9 yolks　2 soupspoons Curaçao
14 egg whites　(butter and flour)

Method: Melt the chocolate over a bain-marie. Stir in the melted butter. Incorporate the yolks and Curaçao. Leave the mixture to cool. Stiffly beat the whites. Fold into the chocolate.

Butter and flour individual soufflé dishes. Chill. Spoon enough soufflé mixture into them to all but fill. Smooth the surface. Ease the chocolate from the edges with the point of a knife. Bake in a hot oven for 8 to 10 minutes.

Note: This recipe is designed for individual servings. It does not work so well when prepared in larger soufflé dishes.

Stephen Ross, of Popjoy's Restaurant, Bath, developed it from the well-loved 'Petit pot au chocolat'.

Poires Meringuées
Pear Meringue Tart

Serves: 8. Total cost: 7 units. Preparation: 40–50 mins. Cooking: pears 40 mins, pastry 25 mins, meringue 10 mins. Oven: pastry 185°C/365°F/Gas Mk 4, meringue 205°C/401°F/Gas Mk 6.

Ingredients　4 pears　*For the pâte sucrée:*
80 g (3 oz) sugar　250 g (9 oz) flour
1 level teaspoon coriander　200 g (7 oz) butter
lemon peel　100 g (3½ oz) castor sugar
vanilla　2 eggs
For the crème pâtissière:　*For the meringue:*
75g (scant 3 oz) flour　3 egg whites
125 g (4 oz) castor sugar　140 g (5 oz) castor sugar
4 yolks
500 ml (17½ fl oz) Jersey milk
vanilla

Method: Peel, halve and core the pears. Poach them in sugar, coriander, peel of half a lemon and four drops of vanilla essence with just enough water to cover.

Boil the milk. Work together flour, sugar, eggs and four drops of vanilla essence. Pour the milk over the mixture. Place in a clean pan and heat. Whisk well as the crème thickens. Strain through a sieve to remove any lumps. Cool.

Crumb the flour and butter. Beat the eggs and sugar. Work the eggs and sugar into the flour and butter to form a paste. Rest. Whisk the whites to stiff peaks. Add half the sugar and continue whisking till the meringue has a gloss on it. Fold in the rest of the sugar.

Butter a large flan ring. Roll out the pâte sucrée. Line the flan ring. Fit a piece of aluminium foil over the paste, pressing in at the edges. Bake blind in a hot oven 15 minutes. Remove the foil and continue baking till crisp.

Spread a layer of crème pâtissière over the pastry. Drain and wipe the pears. Arrange them on the crème. Pipe meringue over the pears. Return to a hot oven for 10 minutes to set the meringue.

Oranges au Whisky
Baked Oranges with Whisky

Serves: 8. Total cost: 5 units. Preparation: 20–25 mins. Cooking: 40 mins. Oven: 175°C/347°F/Gas Mk 4.

Ingredients	
	8 sweet oranges
	60 g (2 oz) almonds
	90 g (3¼ oz) raisins
	500 ml (1¾ fl oz) whisky
	8 teaspoons liquid honey
	30 g (1 oz) butter

Method: Score each orange peel into six segments without cutting the bottom. Blanch the oranges in boiling water for 2 minutes. Peel the oranges, leaving the segments of peel attached to the base of the oranges. Pull apart the segments of orange taking care not to damage the pulp.

Soak the almonds and raisins in whisky for 15 minutes. Stuff the centres of the oranges with them. Fold in the points of peel under the oranges. Arrange the oranges on pieces of buttered foil. Spoon honey over each one. Wrap in foil. Bake in moderate oven for 40 minutes. Serve hot.

Crème Dauphinoise
Walnut and Caramel Cream

Serves: 8. Total cost: 4 units. Preparation: 20–25 mins. Cooking: included in preparation time. Other: chilling 1 hr plus 1 hr.

Ingredients   100 g (3½ oz) granulated sugar
2 soupspoons cornflour
4 eggs
400 ml (14 fl oz) milk
2 soupspoons double cream
15 sugar lumps
125 g (4½ oz) walnuts

Method: Mix together the granulated sugar, 4 yolks, cornflour and milk. Place in a pan over a gentle flame. Whisk until the mixture has thickened.

Prepare a caramel with the sugar lumps. When it starts to change from golden to brown, take it off the flame. Add a teaspoon of water to the caramel. Stir the caramel into the crème. Mix 110 g (4 oz) roughly chopped walnuts into the crème. Chill the crème. Whip the double cream and fold into the crème. Stiffly beat the whites and fold into the crème. Transfer to individual coupes. Chill. Garnish with the remaining chopped walnuts.

Glace au Cognac
Cognac Ice-cream

Serves: 8. Total cost: 8 units. Preparation: 20–25 mins. Other: freezing the ice-cream 6–8 hrs.

Ingredients   220 g (8 oz) vanilla sugar
8 yolks
850 ml (1½ pints) double cream
3 soupspoons cognac

Method: Beat the yolks to the ribbon with the vanilla sugar. (They are ready when the mixture folds like a ribbon as it pours off the whisk.) Whisk the cream with the cognac till it is fairly stiff. Combine with the yolks and sugar. Place in the freezer till on the point of setting. Take out and beat the mixture for 2 minutes. Return to the freezer.

Note: One may turn the ice-cream into an ice-cream soufflé by folding four stiffly beaten whites into the cream before freezing. In this case add a little extra sugar and cognac to compensate for the blandness of the whites. If one overdoes the alcohol in the ice-cream it acts as an anti-freeze.

Menu 3

April–May

First Courses

Main Courses

Sweets

First Courses

Crêpes au Camembert
Pancakes with Camembert

Serves: 8. Total cost: 9 units. Preparation: 15–20 mins. Cooking: 10 mins. Other: macerating camembert 3 hrs, resting batter 1 hr. Oven: 235°C/455°F/Gas Mk 8. Wine suggestion: Mâcon rouge.

Ingredients *For the filling:*
2 ripe camemberts
60 g (2 oz) cream cheese
100 ml (3½ fl oz) white wine
nutmeg
pepper
(butter for baking)
For the crêpes:
165 g (6 oz) flour
2 eggs
300 ml (10 fl oz) milk
pinch of salt
50 g (scant 2 oz) butter

Method: Remove the crusts from the camemberts. Crush them with a fork. Add cream cheese, wine, pepper and nutmeg. Blend together. Leave 3 hours.

Make a pancake batter. Blend together flour, eggs, milk and salt. Rest 1 hour.

Make 16 pancakes. Spoon some of the mixture on each pancake. Roll the pancakes. Brush with butter. Bake 10 minutes in a hot oven.

Jambon Persillé
Ham in a Wine Jelly with Parsley

Serves: 16. Total cost: 12 units. Preparation: 25–35 mins. Cooking: (i) 20 mins, (ii) 2 hrs, (iii) 30 mins. Other: soaking the ham 12 hrs, chilling 12 hrs. Wine suggestion: Beaune.

Ingredients 1 uncooked ham
400 g (14 oz) bacon rinds
3 calves' feet (or pig's trotters)
1 bottle dry white wine
4 onions
4 carrots
1 stick celery
20 peppercorns
6 cloves
bouquet garni
2 eggs
For the jelly:
4 soupspoons cognac
For the herb mixture:
3 cloves garlic
4 shallots
4 soupspoons chopped parsley
2 soupspoons chopped chervil

Method: Soak the ham for 12 hours, changing the water if possible several times. (Place the ham on a rack because the salt will sink to the bottom of the pan.)

Place the ham in a fresh pan of cold water, bring to the boil and simmer for 20 minutes. Remove the ham, rinse and throw out the water. Return the ham to the pan with calves' feet, wine, vegetables, herbs and spices. Add the rinds and enough water to cover the ham. Cover and simmer at the rate of 20 minutes a pound. Once cooked, remove the ham from the heat and allow to cool in its liquor. Remove ham from liquor and reserve.

Strain the bouillon and skim off any surplus fat. Reduce to about 1 litre (1¾ pints). Clarify the bouillon with egg white and shell. Strain as for a consommé. Add cognac.

Mix chopped herbs with crushed garlic and finely chopped shallots. Skin the ham and take it off the bone. Cube the meat. Place a layer of ham in a large terrine. Sprinkle with the herb mixture and moisten with a little cold jelly. Repeat the process and finish with a layer of herbs. Press and level the surface. Pour the jelly on the point of setting over the ham. Serve chilled.

Maquereaux Braisés à la Moutarde

Mackerel Braised with Mustard and Cream

Serves: 8. Total cost: 7 units. Preparation: 25–35 mins. Cooking: fish 15 mins, sauce 5 mins. Wine suggestion: Jurançon.

Ingredients
8 mackerel
100 g (3½ oz) celery
100 g (3½ oz) onion
100 g (3½ oz) carrot
100 g (3½ oz) leek
2 cloves garlic
300 ml (10 fl oz) fish stock
100 ml (3½ fl oz) white wine
150 ml (5 fl oz) double cream
1 soupspoon fennel leaves
1 soupspoon Dijon mustard
1 teaspoon powdered mustard
salt and pepper

Method: Finely dice celery, onion, carrot, leek and garlic. Place them in a pan with stock, white wine, chopped fennel leaves and seasoning. Bring to the boil and simmer 15 minutes. Arrange the mackerel on the bed of vegetables. They should not be covered by the stock. Place a foil lid over the fish. Braise for 10 minutes. Turn over and braise for 5 more minutes.

Arrange vegetables and mackerel on a serving dish and keep warm. Drain the cooking liquor into a fresh pan. Add mustards and cream. Reduce to a coating consistency. Pour over the mackerel. Garnish with chopped fennel leaves.

Oeufs Mousseux à la Tomate

Whisked Eggs with Tomatoes and Cheese

Serves: 8. Total cost 5 units. Preparation: 15–20 mins. Cooking: 15 mins. Oven: 205°C/401°F/Gas Mk 6. Wine suggestion: in accordance with the main course.

Ingredients   8 eggs
500 g (17½ oz) tomatoes
1 medium onion
30 g (1 oz) butter
1 teaspoon Herbes de Provence
1 teaspoon brown sugar
60 g (2 oz) Gruyère
salt and pepper

Method: Dice the onion and fry in butter.

Blanch, peel, pip and dice the tomatoes. Add them to the onion and allow to stew until tender. Add the brown sugar.

Beat the eggs. Season them with herbs, salt and pepper. Stir into the tomato mixture off the heat. Pour the mixture into cassolettes. Dot with finely sliced Gruyère. Bake in a hot oven till set, about 15 minutes.

Quenelles d'Epinards
Spinach Quenelles

Serves: 8. Total cost: 4 units. Preparation: 15–20 mins. Cooking: spinach 15 mins, quenelles 10 mins, gratinating 5 mins. Other: chilling 1 hr. Oven: 235°C/455°F/Gas Mk 8. Wine suggestion: Gewurztraminer.

Ingredients   450 g (1 lb) spinach
350 g (13 oz) curd cheese
1 soupspoon Parmesan
2 yolks
60 g (2 oz) flour
1 teaspoon nutmeg
80 g (3 oz) butter
80 g (3 oz) grated cheese
salt and pepper

Method: Boil the spinach 15 minutes. Drain. Liquidise. Press out as much moisture as possible. Unless this is done thoroughly the quenelles will fall apart.

Combine spinach with curd cheese, Parmesan, yolks, nutmeg and seasoning. Chill, about 1 hour.

103

Spread the flour on a board. Roll spinach mixture in teaspoon-sized balls in the flour. Poach in gently boiling water. The quenelles are ready when they rise to the surface. Place in buttered ovenproof dishes. Brush with melted butter. Sprinkle with grated cheese. Gratinate 5 minutes in a hot oven.

Crème d'Asperges
Fresh Asparagus Soup

Serves: 8. Total cost: 7 units. Preparation: 15 mins. Cooking: asparagus 15 mins, soup 15 mins. Wine suggestion: Moselle – Piesporter.

Ingredients
450 g (1 lb) asparagus
50 g (scant 2 oz) butter
50 g (scant 2 oz) flour
500 ml (17½ fl oz) milk
150 ml (5 fl oz) double cream
2 yolks
salt and pepper

Method: Peel off the leathery skin at the bottom of each asparagus. Tie into a bunch. Perforate an empty 1 kg (2 lb) tin with holes like a colander. Stand the asparagus upright in the tin. Bring a litre of salted water to boil in a steep-sided pan. Drop the asparagus into the pan so that the heads are uncovered by the water. Poach 15 minutes. Cut off the heads, about 3 cm (1¼ in), and reserve for garnish. Liquidise the remainder of the asparagus with a little of their cooking liquid.

Prepare a roux with flour and butter. Add the milk and afterwards the purée of asparagus. Simmer 15 minutes.

Blend the yolks and cream. Whisk into the soup off the heat. Check the seasoning. Garnish with asparagus heads.

Tourte aux Poireaux
Leek and Bacon Pie

Serves: 8. Total cost: 7 units. Preparation: 20–25 mins. Cooking: 45 mins. Oven: 204°/425°F/Gas Mk 7. Wine suggestion: Beaujolais – Villages.

Ingredients 700 g (about 1 ½ lb) feuilletage (page 42)
butter
1 yolk
For the filling:
500 g (17 ½ oz) leeks (trimmed)
500 g (17 ½ oz) potatoes
100 g (3 ½ oz) butter
150 g (5 ½ oz) streaky bacon
parsley
chervil (if available)
salt and pepper

Method: Butter a steep-sided flan dish. Roll out two-thirds of the paste and line the flan dish.

Finely slice the potatoes, about the thickness of an old penny. Finely slice the leeks. Arrange alternate layers of potato and leek on the pastry. Sprinkle each layer with diced bacon, chopped parsley and chervil, pepper and a little salt. Dot cubes of butter on each layer.

Roll out the rest of the pastry. Water the edges and fix the lid to the sides. Cut a hole the size of a ten penny piece in the lid. Make a chimney with pastry trimmings. Fix round the hole. Brush the pastry with egg yolk. Bake in a hot oven 45 minutes.

Filets de Poisson à la Grecque
Marinaded Dabs with Lemon and Spices

Serves: 8. Total cost: 8 units. Preparation: 15–20 mins. Cooking: 20 mins. Other: marinading the fish 2 hrs. Wine suggestion: Sylvaner.

Ingredients

8 dabs skinned and filleted	1 teaspoon tomato purée
2 lemons	½ teaspoon fennel seed
1 onion	½ teaspoon coriander
100 ml (3 ½ fl oz) olive oil	100 ml (3 ½ fl oz) white
2 bayleaves	wine
1 teaspoon marjoram	fennel leaves
400 g (14 ½ oz) tin tomatoes	salt and pepper

Method: Place the fillets in a marinade of wine, oil, bayleaves, marjoram and seasoning. Slice the lemons and add to the marinade. Leave 2 hours, turning the fish after 1 hour.

Bistro Style Cookery

Pour the marinade into a pan. Coarsely chop the onion. Soften in the marinade. Add the fennel seeds, coriander, lemon slices from the marinade, tomato purée and tin of tomatoes. Simmer for 10 minutes uncovered. Place the fillets in the sauce and cover. Simmer for 10 minutes more. Serve garnished with fennel leaves.

Note: One may add a teaspoon of soft brown sugar to the sauce.

Dab fillets are very small. After each fish has been filleted, reform the four fillets before placing in the marinade or the dish will be bitty.

Main Courses

Epaule d'Agneau Sautée aux Aubergines
Lamb Sauté with Aubergines

Serves: 8. Total cost: 20 units. Preparation: 25–35 mins. Cooking: to sauté the lamb about 15 mins. Other: to dégorger the aubergines 1 hr. Wine suggestion: Rosé de Provence.

Ingredients 1 boned shoulder of lamb
100 ml (3½ fl oz) groundnut oil
For the aubergines:
3 aubergines
cooking salt
100 ml (3½ fl oz) groundnut oil
For the sauce:
500 ml (17 fl oz) consommé
100 ml (3½ fl oz) white wine
30 g (1 oz) tomato pureé
1 heaped teaspoon arrowroot
2 soupspoons chopped fresh rosemary
salt and pepper

Method: Peel the aubergines. Cube them (roughly the size of a fingernail). Place them in a colander. Sprinkle with salt. Leave for 1 hour. Press, rinse and wipe the aubergines. Sauté them in hot oil.

Cut the lamb into small pieces, about a mouthful each, after trimming excess fat or gristle. Fry them a few at a time in hot oil. They should be well-coloured on all sides. Set aside and keep warm.

Deglaze the pan in which the lamb has cooked with white wine. Add tomato purée and consommé. Dissolve arrowroot in water. Stir into the sauce. Add the rosemary. Reduce the sauce to a coating consistency. Remove from the heat. Return the lamb and aubergines to the pan. Allow to stand for 2 minutes. Check seasoning, especially pepper.

Note: This is a recipe for lamb. Mutton or hogget even will not do.

Nor should one allow the lamb to stew in the sauce or it will toughen.

109

Porc aux Abricots

Pork with Apricots

Serves: 8. Total cost: 16 units. Preparation: 20–30 mins. Cooking: 45 mins. Other: soaking the apricots 3 hrs. Wine suggestion: Côte Rôtie.

Ingredients   1350 g (about 3 lb) hand of pork
5 onions
350 g (12 oz) dried Turkish apricots
60 g (2 oz) almonds
3 cloves garlic
1 teaspoon each of ginger, coriander, cumin,
    peppercorns, sea salt
100 ml (3½ fl oz) white wine
100 ml (3½ fl oz) groundnut oil

Method: Soak the apricots for a few hours.
Blend the spices in the liquidiser.

Cube the meat. Sauté it in oil. Add sliced onion and garlic. Stir in the spices. When the onion begins to colour deglaze the pan with wine. Add three-quarters of the apricots and the water in which they soaked. Cover and simmer 45 minutes.

Brush the almonds with butter and toast them under the salamander. Garnish the pork with almonds and the rest of the apricots.

Serve with saffron rice (see page 59).

Blanquette de Dinde

Turkey Blanquette

Serves: 12. Total cost: 22 units. Preparation: 20–25 mins. Cooking: 45 mins plus 20 mins. Other: stock 3 hrs. Wine suggestion: Bordeaux – St Julien.

Ingredients   breast meat from a 7 kg (about 16 lb) turkey
2 litres (3 ½ pints) turkey stock
150 g (5 ½ oz) celery
150 g (5 ½ oz) carrot
150 g (5 ½ oz) onion
300 g (11 oz) mushrooms
200 ml (7 fl oz) white wine
1 lemon
thyme
bayleaf
parsley stalks
2 cloves
6 yolks
150 ml (5 fl oz) cream
salt and pepper

Method: Prepare a stock with the turkey carcass, neck and giblets.
Cube the meat into mouthful-sized pieces. Place in cold water. Bring to
the boil. Drain. Place the turkey in a pan with celery, carrot, onion,
thyme, bayleaf, parsley and cloves. Cover with stock and white wine.
Season lightly. Bring to the boil. Cook uncovered for 45 minutes. The
stock will reduce by a third.

Drain the turkey. Place in a fresh pan with mushrooms. Strain
three-quarters of the sauce over the meat. Simmer for 20 minutes more.
Whisk together the remaining stock, the juice of the lemon, the yolks
and the cream.

Incorporate this mixture off the heat into the blanquette. Re-heat gently
to thicken, but do not boil.

Note: Traditionally, one thickened the stock with a roux before the
final 20 minutes cooking. In this case one would use only two yolks at
the end. This method has the advantage of offering a larger margin for
error because one need only whisk in the yolks/cream liaison at the last
minute. However, using no flour the sauce is lighter, more delicate and
has a far better shine.

Cuisses de Dinde Grillées aux Herbes
Turkey Legs Grilled with Herbs

**Serves: 8. Total cost: 17 units. Preparation: 20–30 mins. Cooking:
15 mins. Other: macerating 12 hrs. Oven: 204°C/425°F/Gas Mk 7.
Wine suggestion: Burgundy – Beaune-Grèves.**

111

Ingredients   2 turkey legs from a 7 kg bird (about 16 lb)
100 ml (3½ floz) groundnut oil
2 soupspoons chopped mint
1 soupspoon chives
pepper and sea salt

Method: Bone the turkey legs taking care to remove the sinews. There should be about 1350 g (3 lb) of meat. Cut the legs into 8 portions. Flatten them with a cutlet bat. Brush with oil (or use an oil prepared for grilling). Sprinkle with mint and chives. Season. Wrap in foil and leave overnight.

Grill 5 minutes skinside down (next to the flame). Turn and grill 3 minutes more. Transfer to a hot oven and continue cooking for 7 minutes.

Serve with a butter-compound sauce (Hollandaise, Béarnaise etc.).

Truite au Lard

Trout with Bacon and Red Wine

Serves: 8. Total cost: 27 units. Preparation: 20–25 mins. Cooking: 6 mins, sauce 5 mins. Wine suggestion: Beaujolais – Juliénas.

Ingredients   8 trout
300 g (11 oz) middlecut bacon
4 shallots
400 ml (14 fl oz) red wine
1 soupspoon soft brown sugar
2 soupspoons chopped parsley
50 g (scant 2 oz) butter
flour
salt and pepper

Method: Cut the bacon into lardons. Blanch for 5 minutes. Drain. Mince the shallots. Heat the butter. Fry the lardons till they are golden. Set aside.

Season the trout. Pass them through seasoned flour. Fry them in the pan used for the bacon. Transfer to a serving dish and keep warm.

Return bacon to the pan. Add shallots and brown sugar. Deglaze with wine and reduce rapidly till the sauce has glazed. Stir in the parsley. Pour sauce and bacon over the trout.

Filets de St Pierre au Fromage de Basilic

John Dory Fillets with Basil and Cottage Cheese

Serves: 8. Total cost: 22 units. Preparation: 15–25 mins. Cooking: 10 mins. Other: chilling cheese 1 hr. Wine suggestion: Gewurztraminer.

Ingredients   8 small John Dory
2 eggs
100 g (3 ½ oz) white breadcrumbs
100 g (3 ½ oz) flour
110 g (4 oz) unsalted butter
30 g (1 oz) fresh basil leaves
1 teaspoon chopped parsley
½ clove garlic
½ lemon
110 g (4 oz) cottage cheese
salt and pepper

Method: Fillet and skin the John Dory (2 fillets per fish). Dip them in seasoned flour, egg and breadcrumbs.

Blend the cottage cheese with lemon juice, garlic, salt and pepper. Break up three-quarters of the basil leaves by hand (chopping discolours the leaves). Stir into the cheese together with parsley. Chill, about 1 hour. hour.

Heat the butter in a pan. Shallow-fry the fillets (about 5 minutes each side). Garnish with remaining basil leaves.

Serve sauce separately like a sauce tartare.

Matelote au Riesling

Fish Stew with Riesling

Serves: 8. Total cost: 22 units. Preparation: 25–35 mins. Cooking: 30 mins plus, depends on the fish being used. Other: soaking eel 1 hr, other fish less time depending on texture. Wine suggestion: Riesling.

H

Ingredients   1600 g (about 3½ lb) eels, carp, bream or a mixture of
all three
250 g (9 oz) middle cut bacon
1 large onion
250 g (9 oz) carrot
60 g (2 oz) butter
60 g (2 oz) flour
2 bayleaves
thyme
1 bunch of parsley
75 ml (2½ fl oz) cream
milk
50 g (scant 2 oz) butter (for the fish)
700 ml (1 bottle) Riesling
salt and pepper

Method: Dice the onion. Cut the bacon into lardons. Cut the carrot
into julienne. Sweat carrot, onion and bacon in butter. Stir in flour.
Moisten with the Riesling. Add the thyme, bayleaves and parsley stalks.
Bring to the boil and simmer covered for 30 minutes.

Soak the fish in milk, 5 cm (2 in) pieces of eel or fillets of any other fish.
Stew the fish for 10 minutes in butter. Transfer to the matelote.
Continue cooking uncovered till the fish is tender. Add the cream.
Check seasoning. Garnish with chopped parsley.

Note: The author recently came across a recipe for a matelote
(6 covers) using 6 bottles of Côtes du Rhône which simmered all day
till reduced to about a litre. Such practice might seem a little excessive
to most English cooks, even out and out Francophiles.

Paupiettes Normande
Veal Paupiettes with Apples and Cream

**Serves 8. Total cost: 29 units. Preparation: 50–60 mins. Cooking:
20 mins, sauce 10 mins. Other: chilling the forcemeat 1 hr. Wine
suggestion: Bordeaux – Pauillac.**

Ingredients   16 paupiettes (see page 33)   300 ml (10 fl oz)
For the sauce: double cream
500 g (18 oz) eating apples   25 ml (1 fl oz) Calvados
50 g (scant 2 oz) butter   60 g (2 oz) celery
300 ml (10 fl oz) apple juice   salt and pepper

Method: Prepare the paupiettes as described on page 33. Peel, core and slice the apples. Fry them in butter till they have coloured on both sides. Set aside.

Deglaze the pan with apple juice. Add finely diced celery and reduce rapidly. Pour juices from the cooked paupiettes into the pan. Continue the reduction. When only a quarter of the original liquid remains, add the Calvados. Then add the cream and continue reducing. Return the apples to the pan. Season.

Coat paupiettes with the sauce and garnish with apples.

Brochettes Zingara
Rump Steak Kebabs with Pepperonata

Serves: 8. Total cost: 22 units. Preparation: 20–30 mins. Cooking: meat 5 mins, garnish 15 mins. Other: marinading 1 hr. Wine suggestion Provence – Bandol, Côte du Rhône – Châteauneuf du Pape.

Ingredients

1200 g (42 oz) trimmed rump steak	30 g (1 oz) butter
200 g (14 oz) lean bacon	200 ml (7 fl oz) grilling oil
8 green peppers	30 g (1 oz) paprika
2 lemons	fresh bayleaves
	salt and pepper

Method: Cut the beef into 2½ cm (1 in) cubes. Let them marinade for 1 hour in the oil seasoned with paprika and bayleaves. (Do not marinade for more than 1 hour or the flavour of bayleaves will dominate.)

Zest the lemons and divide the zests into as many pieces as there are pieces of meat. Squeeze the juice and set aside.

Cube the bacon. Soften in butter.

Chop the peppers into similar sized bâtons. Sweat for 10 minutes with the bacon. Add the lemon juice and simmer 5 minutes longer.

Place the meat on skewers alternating meat with zests. Start and finish with a bayleaf. Grill for about 5 minutes, using the marinade to baste the brochettes. Season.

Serve with the peppers and bacon as an accompaniment.

Sweets

Crème Brûlée
Cream with Caramelised Brown Sugar

Serves: 8. Total cost: 10 units. Preparation: 10–15 mins. Cooking: 50 mins. Other: glazing 3 mins. Oven: 160°C/320°F/Gas Mk 2.

Ingredients 800 ml (28 fl oz) double cream
4 eggs
4 yolks
100 g (3½ oz) castor sugar
demerara sugar
vanilla essence

Method: Heat the cream with a few drops of vanilla essence. Mix the eggs, yolks and castor sugar. Pour the cream over them. Beat. Strain. Pour a quantity of cream into eight ramekin dishes. Put the dishes in a bain-marie and bake in a low oven to set. Chill.

Spread an even layer of brown sugar over each cream; it has to be even or the caramel will be cooked in one part and not another. Place ramekin dishes under a hot salamander. Caramelise to dark amber. Allow 3 minutes to set and cool.

Pommes en Douillons
Apples Baked in a Wine Pastry

Serves: 8. Total cost: 8 units. Preparation: 30 mins. Cooking: 30 mins. Other: rest paste 2 hrs. Oven: 205°C/401°F/Gas Mk 6.

Ingredients 4 large eating apples
600 g (21 oz) flour
200 ml (7 fl oz) white wine
30 g (1 oz) castor sugar
350 g (12 oz) butter
cinnamon
soft brown sugar
1 egg
For the cream:
200 ml (7 fl oz) double cream
30 g (1 oz) castor sugar
1 soupspoon Calvados

Method: Slightly warm the wine. Whisk the softened butter into it a few pieces at at time. Off the heat, add castor sugar and flour. Work the paste into a ball. Rest for 2 hours.

Peel, halve and core the apples. Dust them with a mixture of brown sugar and cinnamon.

Divide the dough into 8 equal portions. Roll out. Place the apple on each piece. Wrap like apple dumplings. Brush with egg yolk. Bake in a hot oven 30 minutes.

Whip the cream with the Calvados and sugar.

Tarte aux Noix et au Miel
Honey and Walnut Tart

Serves: 8. Total cost: Preparation: 35–45 mins. Cooking: 25 mins. Other: resting pastry 30 mins, soaking walnuts 2 hrs. Oven: 220°C/428°F/Gas Mk 7.

Ingredients
250 g (9 oz) walnuts
150 g (5 ½ oz) liquid honey
For the crème:
80 g (3 oz) sugar
60 g (2 oz) flour
4 yolks
300 ml (10 fl oz) Jersey milk
vanilla essence
For the pâte sablée:
250 g (9 oz) flour
150 g (5 ½ oz) butter
pinch of salt
1 large egg
70 g (scant 3 oz) sugar
(butter for flan ring)

Method: Soak the walnuts in honey for 2 hours. Make a crème pâtissière. Beat sugar, yolks and flour. Pour over hot milk. Mix well. Transfer to a fresh pan. Bring to the boil stirring regularly. Take the crème off the heat as soon as it has thickened. Add four drops of vanilla essence. Cool.

Make a pâte sablée. Crumb the flour, salt and butter. Mix the egg and sugar. Work into the flour and butter. Roll into a ball. Rest 30 minutes.

Butter a flan ring. Line with pastry. Bake blind in a hot oven 15
minutes. Remove the baking beans or foil. Continue baking a further 10
minutes.

Spread the crème over the tart case. Drain the walnuts. Arrange on the
crème. Cover the edges of the tart with foil. Place the tart under a hot
salamander (i.e. grill) for 4 minutes. Cool.

Sorbet aux Poires
Pear Sorbet with Poached Pears

**Serves: 8. Total cost: 5 units. Preparation: 20–25 mins. Cooking:
40 mins. Other: cooling pear purée 1 hr, freezing pear sorbet 24
hrs.**

Ingredients   1 ½ kg (about 3 ½ lb) ripe pears (Williams or Bartlett's)
170 g (6 oz) vanilla sugar
peel of 1 orange
½ teaspoon nutmeg
1 clove
1 pinch ginger
25 ml (1 fl oz) Kirsch or pear eau-de-vie
2 egg whites

Method: Peel, halve and core the pears. Place them in a pan with
sugar, peel, nutmeg, clove, and ginger. Cover with water. Bring to the
boil and poach till tender, about 40 minutes. Remove eight pear
segments and all but 300 ml (10 fl oz) syrup. Chill the pear segments
with their juice. Liquidise the pears left in the pan. Pass them through a
sieve or chinois. Cool. Add the Kirsch.

Whisk the whites to soft peaks. Fold into the purée. Pour into the
ice-cream machine. Freeze. Serve the sorbet with pear segments and a
little juice.

Note: If one does not have an ice-cream making machine, place the
purée in the freezer minus the whites till on the point of setting.
Remove, beat for 2 minutes, fold in the whites and return to the freezer.
Pear sorbet unlike a syrup-based sorbet will go hard if left in a freezer
more than 24 hours. In this case transfer to a fridge during service.

Marquise au Chocolat
Chocolate Marquise

**Serves: 8. Total cost: 8 units. Preparation: 20–25 mins.
Other: to set 12 hrs.**

Ingredients   350 g (12 oz) plain chocolate
160 g (6 oz) unsalted butter
100 g (3 ½ oz) castor sugar
4 eggs
50 ml (scant 2 fl oz) crème de menthe
150 ml (5 fl oz) double cream

Method: Melt the chocolate in a bain-marie. Cream the yolks and butter. Mix a soupspoon of hot water into the chocolate. Stir in the yolks and butter. Add half the crème de menthe.

Stiffly beat the whites. Fold into the chocolate mixture as soon as it has cooled. Place in a buttered mould and leave to set overnight.

Whip the cream and sugar with rest of the crème de menthe. Turn out the Marquise au Chocolat. Decorate it with piped cream.

Menu 4

May–June

First Courses

Main Courses

Sweets

First Courses

Brochettes de Crevettes Piri-piri

Prawn Kebabs with Chilli and Sherry Condiment

Serves: 8. Total cost: 7 units. Preparation: 10–15 mins. Cooking: 3 mins. Other: marinading the chillis. Wine suggestion: Chablis.

Ingredients   6 dozen prawns
2 chillis
150 ml (5 fl oz) dry sherry
220 g (8 oz) butter
grilling oil

Method: Mince the chillis. Add them to the sherry. Soak as long as possible.

Remove the heads and the top half of the shell on the prawns. Place the prawns on skewers.

Liquidise the heads with the chillis and sherry. Strain into a fresh pan. Heat, but do not bring to the boil. Divide the softened butter into knobs. Whisk into the liquid.

Brush the brochettes with oil. Grill about 3 minutes.

Serve the sauce separately.

Note: One may prepare a condiment with sherry and chillis to taste which improves with age and keeps almost indefinitely. It is excellent in soups, especially turkey or game.

Langues au Roquefort

Lambs' Tongues with a Roquefort Dressing

Serves: 8. Total cost: 10 units. Preparation: 15–20 mins. Cooking: blanching 20 mins, simmering 1½ hrs. Other: soaking 2 hrs. Wine suggestion: Bordeaux Superieur.

Ingredients   8 sheep's tongues
2 onions
2 carrots
500 ml (17 fl oz) consommé
75 ml (about 3 fl oz) groundnut oil
25 ml (about 1 fl oz) wine vinegar
1 teaspoon chopped parsley
100 g (3½ oz) Roquefort
bouquet garni
salt and pepper

Method: Soak the tongues in cold water for 2 hours. Blanch them in boiling water for 20 minutes.

Place them in a fresh pan with roughly chopped onion, carrot and bouquet garni. Cover with consommé and an equal quantity of water. Simmer for 90 minutes. Check seasoning. Drain, skin and slice.

Blend the oil, vinegar and Roquefort, seasoned with pepper only.

Arrange the tongue on individual dishes. Pour over the Roquefort cream. Garnish with parsley.

Note: Keep the lamb out of the cold room or fridge or it will harden.

Crabe Pen'march
Breton Dressed Crab

Serves: 8. Total cost: 12 units. Preparation: 30–40 mins. Cooking: 20 mins. Wine suggestion: Muscadet.

Ingredients   8 small crabs
1 litre (35 fl oz) fish stock
300 ml (10 fl oz) mayonnaise
2 red pimentoes
2 sprigs of mint
salt and cayenne pepper

Method: Plunge the uncooked crabs in boiling salted fish stock. Poach for 20 minutes.

Drain. Flake the meat from legs, claws etc. into a bowl.

Add the chopped mint and red pepper (previously blanched, skinned, pipped and diced). Stir in the mayonnaise. Add a pinch of cayenne to the mixture.

Fill the shells with the mixture.

Note: Once the summer has started and fresh herbs are readily available it is tempting to be heavy-handed with their use. Crab is a delicately flavoured meat. Large quantities of dill, tarragon, fennel or chervil will overpower the taste.

It goes almost without saying that one should use live crabs, not those that have been boiled by the local fishmonger.

As an alternative to fish stock one may boil them in sea-water if one is by the seaside. Place the crabs on a rack inside the pan.

Potage de Concombre à la Menthe
Iced Cucumber and Mint Soup

Serves: 8. Total cost: 6 units. Preparation: 15–20 mins. Cooking 10 mins. Other: chilling the soup 3 hrs. Wine suggestion: in accordance with main course, though Moselle would suit.

Ingredients
2 cucumbers
160 g (6 oz) potato
50 g (scant 2 oz) butter
600 ml (1 pint) milk
600 ml (1 pint) chicken stock
7 good sprigs fresh mint
150 ml (5 fl oz) double cream
salt and pepper

Method: Dice the potato. Sweat in the butter. Peel and coarsely chop the cucumbers. Put them in the pan with the potato. Pour over the stock and milk. Tie the mint together. Keep back a few of the top leaves for garnishing. Add the mint to the pan. Season. Bring to the boil. Simmer 10 minutes till the cucumber is tender. Cool. Blend in the liquidiser after removing the bunch of mint. Chill. Stir in the cream. Garnish with shredded mint leaves.

Crème d'Artichauts
Cream of Globe Artichoke Soup

Serves: 8. Total cost: 8 units. Preparation: 35–45 mins. Cooking: 30 mins. Wine suggestion: in accordance with main course.

Ingredients
8 artichokes
1 lemon
100 ml (3½ fl oz) white wine
1 large onion
25 ml (about ¾ fl oz) groundnut oil
40 g (1½ oz) flour
50 g (scant 2 oz) butter
150 ml (5 fl oz) cream
2 yolks
salt and pepper

Method: Remove the stalks of the artichokes and the outside leaves. Trim the top leaves with kitchen scissors.

Bring 2 litres (3½ pints) salted water to the boil. Brush each artichoke with the lemon juice. Add the remaining lemon juice and groundnut oil to the boiling water.

Boil the artichokes 30 minutes. Drain. Peel all the outer leaves and return to the pan. Keep the hearts for garnishing the Ris de Veau (see page 141). Allow the liquid to cool.

Place the leaves and liquid together in a liquidiser. Blend as far as possible. The leaves will not liquidise, but the flavour will be imparted to the liquid. Strain the liquid.

Make a roux with the flour and butter. Dice the onion and add to the roux. Moisten with the stock from the artichokes. Add the wine, cream and seasoning. Finish by whisking in the yolks off the heat.

Note: One needs to be ruthless in choosing artichokes for this soup. If the leaves are at all splayed, it is likely that the artichoke is old and liable to be on the bitter side.

Terrine Paysanne
Pork Terrine with Olives

Serves: 10. Total cost: 11 units. Preparation: 15–20 mins. Cooking: 1½ hrs. Other: cooling 1 hr, resting 24 hrs. Oven: 190°C/374°F/Gas Mk 5. Wine suggestion: Tavel rosé.

Ingredients
400 g (14 oz) minced belly of pork
350 g (12 oz) minced veal
100 g (3½ oz) ham
1 large clove garlic
300 g (10 oz) stoned green olives
2 eggs
2 soupspoons tarragon vinegar
100 ml (3½ fl oz) eau-de-vie (or Spanish brandy)
2 soupspoons chopped parsley
1 teaspoon olive oil
3 bayleaves
nutmeg
salt and pepper
1 piece bacon rind
(flour and water paste)

Method: Chop the ham. Combine the meats. Add parsley, chopped garlic and nutmeg. Lightly beat egg with tarragon vinegar and eau-de-vie. Blend into the farce. Season with salt and a generous amount of pepper. (Pepper tends to lose its flavour during cooking so, especially with a pâté, one needs to put more than one's instinct inclines one to.) Allow to stand overnight.

Oil the bottom of a terrine. Place a large piece of bacon rind on top with a bayleaf under it. Spread a layer of farce in the terrine. Arrange half the olives on top. Repeat and finish with a layer of farce. Place remaining bay leaves on top. Seal the lid with a flour and water paste. Place in a bain-marie and bake in a moderate oven for 1½ hours.

Take from the oven. Cool for 1 hour. Remove lid and weight. Leave for 24 hours before serving.

Tourte Bourguignonne
Burgundy Pork Pie

Serves: 8. Total cost: 11 units. Preparation: 50–60 mins. Cooking: jelly 45 mins, tourte 45 mins. Other: marinading 2 hrs. Oven: 200°C/392°F/Gas Mk 6. Wine suggestion: Corton.

Ingredients	400 g (14 oz) flour
	220 g (8 oz) butter
	2 large eggs
	1 yolk
	500 g (18 oz) lean pork
	500 ml (17 fl oz) white wine
	2 onions
	1 clove garlic
	3 juniper berries
	1 bayleaf
	1 bunch of thyme
	2 soupspoons brandy
	1 calf's foot (or 2 leaves gelatine)
	salt and pepper
	(butter and flour)

Method: Prepare a rich shortcrust paste. Crumb the flour and butter. Beat in the whole eggs. Roll into a ball and rest.

Slice the pork into collops. Place in a marinade of white wine, brandy, onion, garlic, herbs and spices. For the best result one should leave it overnight.

Butter and flour a pie dish. Line with the pastry, setting aside enough for the lid. Fill with the pork. Season. Roll out the remaining paste for the lid. Prepare a chimney in the centre of the tourte using card or a piece of surplus paste. Brush with egg yolk. Bake in a moderately hot oven for 45 minutes.

Meanwhile, transfer the marinade to a fresh pan, add the calf's foot and simmer uncovered for 45 minutes. (If using gelatine, soak the leaves while the marinade is simmering, dissolve and add to the reduced liquor.)

Pour the marinade on to the tourte through the chimney. Allow to cool at room temperature. Leave several hours to set.

Fricadelles de Veau à la Graisse Normande
Medallions of Veal Forcemeat Baked in a Piece of Sirloin

Serves: 8. Total cost: 9 units. Preparation: 35–45 mins. Cooking: graisse 1½ hrs, fricadelles 25 mins. Other: Re-heating 10 mins. Oven: 204°C/425°F/Gas Mk 7. Wine suggestion: Bordeaux – St Emilion.

Ingredients   *For the 'graisse':*
100 g (3½ oz) lard
100 g (3½ oz) beef suet
200 g (7 oz) mirepoix (carrots, onion, celery leaves and leek)
1 teaspoon chopped sage
1 large bouquet garni
salt and pepper
For the 'fricadelles':
400 g (14 oz) veal (any cheap cut)
60 g (2 oz) onion
30 g (1 oz) chopped parsley
100 g (3½ oz) white bread soaked in milk and squeezed
1 large egg
salt and pepper
180 g (6 oz) trimmed sirloin steak

I

Method: Prepare the graisse. Place all the first set of ingredients in a pan. Heat very gently and allow the vegetables to stew in the fat for 1½ hours. The aim is to impart the flavour of vegetables and herbs to the fat. Strain and set.

Blend the veal, onion, bread, parsley, egg, graisse and seasoning till they form a perfectly smooth mixture. Roll to form a piece of piping about 30 cm (12 in) long.

Tap out the sirloin till it is large enough to envelop the veal. Wrap in foil. Cook in a hot oven 25 minutes. Cool.

Slice the rolled fricadelle into discs (four slices per person). Re-heat, brushing with a little fat rendered during the first cooking. Serve with a Béarnaise sauce.

Main Courses

Tagine à l'Algérienne
Spiced Stewed Lamb

Serves: 8. Total cost: 25 units. Preparation: 30–40 mins. Cooking: 5 hrs. Other: soaking the chick peas 12 hrs. Wine suggestion: quality Algerian red e.g. Mascara.

Ingredients
1 leg of hogget
3 large onions
3 carrots
450 g (1 lb) tinned tomatoes
60 g (2 oz) mutton fat
2 litres (3 ½ pints) chicken stock
200 g (7 oz) chick peas
For the seasoning:
1 sachet saffron
2 teaspoons ginger
1 ½ teaspoons cumin
1 teaspoon allspice
½ teaspoon nutmeg
½ teaspoon turmeric
8 hulled cardamon seeds
2 cloves
½ teaspoon fennel seeds
2 bayleaves
4 whole cloves garlic
1 (possibly 2) chilli
sea salt
(flour and water paste)

Method: Soak the chick peas overnight.

Bone the meat. Cut it into large cubes. Fry in mutton fat till well coloured on all sides. One may fry the bones as well. Drain off the fat in the bottom of the pan.

Roughly chop onions and carrots. Add them to the pan with tomatoes and chick peas. Pour over the chicken stock.

Blend all the seasonings in the liquidiser with the exception of the bayleaves, chilli and garlic.

Add the spices, garlic, chilli and bayleaves to the pan. Bring to the boil.

Prepare a flour and water paste, the consistency of putty. Seal the lid to the pan with a ribbon of paste around the outer edge. Place in a low oven. Simmer for 5 hours.

Note: This dish will be better re-heated, especially the flavour of the meat.

Tagines of one kind or another are the natural accompaniment of couscous, which the Algerians and French colonials brought from North Africa. Couscous itself is available in England though not easy to obtain. To cook, one soaks it in salted water till it swells, about 5 minutes, and then one steams it till it heats through.

A spiced rice dish (see page 59) is an acceptable accompaniment if one cannot find couscous.

Côtelette de Porc en Papillote
Pork Baked with Tarragon, Sage and Vegetables

Serves: 8. Total cost: 16 units. Preparation: 25–35 mins. Cooking: 17 mins. Other: macerating 2 hrs. Oven: 204°C/425°F/Gas Mk 7. Wine suggestion: Bordeaux – red Graves.

Ingredients   8 large trimmed pork chops
250 g (9 oz) carrot
250 g (9 oz) leek
1 soupspoon dried sage
1 soupspoon chopped rosemary
1 soupspoon chopped chives
salt and pepper

Method: Rub the pork both sides with salt. Season generously with freshly ground pepper and rosemary. Leave 2 hours.

Boil a pint of water. Add salt and dry sage. Simmer 5 minutes.

Slice the carrot and leek in a julienne dice. Drop the carrot in the simmering water. Leave 4 minutes then add the leek. Simmer a further 4 minutes. Drain the carrot and leek.

Arrange each cutlet on a piece of buttered foil. Spread the julienne over the meat. Sprinkle with chopped chives and rosemary. Seal the foil. Bake in a hot oven 17 minutes.

Note: Though this dish does not qualify as 'Cuisine Minceur', one should follow Michel Guérard's advice regarding dishes 'en papillote'. Open the foil under the nose of the customer so he obtains full benefit of the aroma.

Grillade de Veau à la Ratatouille de Poivrons

Veal Minced with Herbs, served with Pepper Ratatouille

Serves: 8. Total cost: 22 units. Preparation: ratatouille 15–20 mins, veal 15–20 mins. Cooking: veal 8 mins, ratatouille 15 mins. Wine suggestion: Tavel rosé.

Ingredients   1400 g (50 oz) shoulder of veal
1 teaspoon chopped tarragon
1 teaspoon chopped mint
1 soupspoon thyme
1 soupspoon grated orange zests
salt and pepper
grilling oil

Method: Trim the veal of all fat and sinew. Put twice through the mincer. Season. Add the chopped tarragon and mint. Form into steaks less than 2½ cm (1 in) thick.

Brush the grill with grilling oil. Place the thyme and orange zests on top. When they begin to smoke, brush the veal steaks with oil and grill rapidly.

If one uses a charcoal grill, use sprigs of thyme and peeled zests.

Ingredients   *For the ratatouille de poivrons:*
1 kg (2¼ lb) peppers
450 g (1 lb) tomatoes
450 g (1 lb) onions
100 ml (3½ fl oz) groundnut oil
salt and pepper
1 teaspoon vinegar

Method: Blanch, peel and pip the peppers and the tomatoes.

Slice the onions into rings. Sweat them in oil till they are transparent.

Dice the tomato. Slice the peppers into strips. Add the peppers to the pan with the onion. Cover and stew for 10 minutes. Uncover. Add the tomato, vinegar, salt and pepper. Cover again and stew for 5 minutes more. Uncover. Turn up the flame and continue till any liquid in the pan has evaporated.

Suprême de Volaille à l'Estragon
Stuffed Breast of Chicken with Tarragon Sauce

Serves: 8. Total cost: 21 units. Preparation: 45–60 mins. Cooking: 20 mins, sauce 10 mins. Oven: 235°C/455°F/Gas Mk 8. Wine suggestion: Burgundy – Montrachet.

Ingredients
8 chicken breasts
220 g (8 oz) butter
salt and pepper
For the farce:
250 (9 oz) shallots
250 g (9 oz) mushrooms
40 g (1 ½ oz) butter
1 teaspoon powdered tarragon
1 slice white bread
1 egg
salt and pepper
(milk)
For the sauce:
150 ml (5 fl oz) cream
150 ml (5 fl oz) white wine
150 ml (5 fl oz) chicken stock
2 yolks
50 g (scant 2 oz) butter
2 soupspoons chopped fresh tarragon

Method: Remove the fillets from the chicken breasts. Brush them with oil and tap them out lightly with a cutlet bat between two sheets of greaseproof paper. Set aside.

Using the point of a sharp knife, cut along the thick side of the breasts to make pockets for the stuffing.

Sweat the diced shallots in the butter. When they have softened add the sliced mushrooms. Cook for 5 minutes. Cool. Soak the bread in milk. Squeeze out the moisture. Blend with the egg, powdered tarragon and seasoning. Combine with the shallots and mushrooms.

Spread some farce in each pocket of breast. Spread the remainder on top. Cover the top layer of farce with the flattened fillets. Season. Wrap each breast in buttered greaseproof paper. Bake in a hot oven 20 minutes.

To make the sauce, reduce the wine and stock by two-thirds. Add the cream and continue the reduction. Before the sauce reaches a coating consistency stir in the tarragon. Add the yolks off the heat. Whisk in knobs of softened butter. Coat the suprêmes with the sauce. Glaze under the salamander.

Boeuf à la Bourgeoise
Ragout of Beef in Red Wine with Onions

Serves: 8. Total cost: 13 units. Preparation: 25–35 mins. Cooking: 1¼ hrs, plus 1¼ hrs. Other: marinading 3 hrs. Wine suggestion: V.D.Q.S. Roussillon.

Ingredients   1350 g (3 lb) chuck steak in a piece
500 ml (17 fl oz) white wine
150 g (5 ½ oz) smoked bacon
100 ml (3 ½ fl oz) groundnut oil
100 g (3 ½ oz) carrot
100 g (3 ½ oz) onion
bouquet garni
1 teaspoon allspice
1 teaspoon paprika
salt and pepper
For the second stage:
450 g (1 lb) carrots
24 button onions

Method: Cut the meat into pieces about 100 g (3 ½ oz) each.

Roll the bacon (cut into strips) in a mixture of paprika and allspice. Lard the meat with the strips of bacon. Marinade in the wine for 3 hours.

Heat the oil. Fry the pieces of larded beef in the oil till well coloured. Add the roughly chopped onion and carrot to the pan. Allow them to colour. Arrange the meat on a bed of vegetables. Pour over the marinade. Add the bouquet garni and some seasoning. Cover and braise for 1¼ hours. The meat should be turned half way through this first cooking. Add extra stock if necessary.

Peel and slice the carrots. Peel the button onions. Place the meat in a fresh pan with them.

Cool the braising liquor. Skim off excess fat. Blend liquor in a liquidiser. Pass the stock over the meat. Cover. Braise for a further 1¼ hours. Check the seasoning, especially the pepper.

137

Rouget Grillé à la Ravigote
Red Mullet Grilled with a Hot Ravigote Sauce

Serves: 8. Total cost: 20 units. Preparation: 15–25 mins. Cooking: 6 mins. Wine suggestion: Burgundy – Rully.

Ingredients 8 red mullet
grilling oil (see page 32)
salt and pepper
For the sauce ravigote:
150 ml (5 fl oz) olive oil
50 ml (1¾ fl oz) white wine vinegar
2 teaspoons capers
50 g (scant 2 oz) onions
1 soupspoon chopped chives
1 soupspoon chopped parsley
1 soupspoon chopped fennel leaves
1 soupspoon chopped tarragon
salt and pepper

Method: Prepare the sauce. Chop the capers and onion. Add them to the herbs. Mix the oil and vinegar as for a vinaigrette. Incorporate the herbs, capers, onion, salt and pepper. Place in a pan and heat gently. Warm, but do not cook.

Clean the mullet, leaving in the liver. Season. Wipe thoroughly. Brush with oil. Grill rapidly, about 3 minutes each side. Spoon a little of the sauce over each fish. Serve the rest of the sauce separately.

Note: Faced with the difficult problem of regular supply of red mullet, one may, if necessary, replace them with gurnards, grey mullet or even whiting.

Colin en Gelée à la Mayonnaise de Homard
Hake in Jelly with Lobster Mayonnaise

Serves: 8. Total cost: 26 units. Preparation: 50–60 mins. Cooking: hake 10 mins, lobster 20 mins. Wine suggestion: Burgundy – Montrachet.

Ingredients   *For the colin:*
8 × 180 g (6 oz) hake steaks
1 litre (1 ¾ pints) fish stock
2 egg whites
220 g (8 oz) prawns for garnish
1 lemon
dill (or fennel)
salt and pepper

Method: Bring the fish stock to the boil. Season. Poach the steaks of hake for 10 minutes (they should have been cut from the middle of the fish). Drain. Cool.

Reduce the stock by two-thirds. Cool a little of the stock. Lightly beat with the whites. Add the juice of a lemon to the stock. Stir the whites into the stock. Return to the boil. Simmer very gently for 30 minutes. Strain the clarified 'fumet' through a fine-meshed sieve or muslin. Chill.

Place the hake on a cooling rack. When the fish jelly is on the point of setting, coat each steak twice with the jelly. Dip the prawns in the jelly and decorate the steaks. Arrange a sprig of fresh dill (or fennel) on each steak. Brush with jelly.

Ingredients   *For the mayonnaise:*
1 small lobster (under 1 lb)
150 ml (5 fl oz) fish stock
150 ml (5 fl oz) white wine
100 ml (3 ½ fl oz) olive oil
1 soupspoon cognac
4 yolks
1 lemon
250 ml (8 ½ fl oz) olive oil
250 ml (8 ½ fl oz) groundnut oil
1 stick of celery
chopped dill
salt and pepper

Method: Boil the lobster 20 minutes in the seasoned stock and wine. Drain. Dice the meat. Moisten with cognac. Pound the shell in a mortar with the 100 ml (3 ½ fl oz) olive oil. Strain through muslin or a fine sieve.

Prepare a mayonnaise. Whisk the 250 ml (8 ½ fl oz) olive oil, the groundnut and the 'lobster oil', a little at a time into the yolks. Season with lemon juice, salt and pepper. Dice the celery and add to the mayonnaise. Add the dill. Add the diced lobster meat. Serve as an accompaniment to the hake.

Note: Instead of using steaks of fish, one may poach a large hake whole. The result will look much more attractive, but may cause more problems during service. The first and second portions served will be fine, but pity the customer who has the last piece.

Ballottine de Volaille Lucullus
Chicken Legs Stuffed with Gammon

Serves: 8. Total cost: 16 units. Preparation: 35–45 mins. Cooking: 5 mins, plus 10 mins. Other: soaking and blanching gammon 1¼ hrs. Oven: 204°C/425°F/Gas Mk 7. Wine suggestion: Beaujolais – Chiroubles.

Ingredients
8 chicken legs
250 g (9 oz) gammon
1 teaspoon chopped chives
1 teaspoon chopped parsley
1 large egg
2 slices bread soaked in milk and squeezed dry
salt and pepper
grilling oil

Method: Bone the chicken legs without damaging meat or skin.

Soak the gammon in water for 1 hour. Blanch 15 minutes. Mince. Prepare a farce with the minced gammon, parsley, chives, bread, lightly beaten egg and seasoning.

Spread a little of the farce on each leg. Roll up as near to the original shape as possible. Fasten the edges with a cocktail stick. Brush with grilling oil. Grill for 5 minutes with the skin next to the heat. Transfer to an oiled baking tray and finish cooking in a hot oven, about 10 minutes.

Serve with a butter compound sauce, Béarnaise or Hollandaise.

Note: As an alternative to grilling, one may wrap the legs in cooking film or foil and bake in the oven.

Ris de Veau aux Coeurs d'Artichauts
Veal Sweetbreads with Artichoke Hearts

Serves: 8. Total cost: 21 units. Preparation: 35–45 mins. Cooking: 40 mins, sauce 5 mins. Other: soaking the sweetbreads 2 hrs. Wine suggestion: Bordeaux – Margaux.

Ingredients
1500 g (about 3½ lb) veal sweetbreads (see Note)
350 g (12 oz) middle cut bacon
1 clove garlic
1 medium onion
200 ml (7 fl oz) white wine
30 g (1 oz) butter
200 ml (7 fl oz) cream
bouquet garni
8 poached artichoke hearts (see page 126)
salt and pepper

Method: Soak the sweetbreads in cold water for 2 hours, changing the water regularly. Rinse them under running water. Place them in a pan with water to cover. Bring to the boil and drain. Remove as much of the skin as possible. Place them between two large trays and weight for 30 minutes.

Roughly dice three-quarters of the bacon. Slice the remainder into fine strips. Use these to lard the sweetbreads.

Dice the onion. Sweat the onion and bacon in butter in a sauteuse 5 minutes. Add the garlic, bouquet garni and white wine. Place the sweetbreads on a bed of bacon and onion. Season lightly. Cover and stew for 40 minutes. Baste regularly.

Remove the lid. Pour over the cream. Boil and reduce to a coating consistency.

Dice the artichoke hearts into small cubes. Stir into the sauce. Leave them just long enough to heat through. Serve.

Note: The sweetbreads that most butchers, especially the provincial ones, sell are what the French call 'animelles' and come from the tail end. These are pleasantly flavoured, but if one does not want to be brought before a Trades Description Tribunal call them by their right name. A set of sweetbreads will weigh around a pound. The 'animelles' weigh 60–90 g (2–3 oz) each and are less tender.

Sweets

Oranges Meknes
Orange and Date Salad

Serves: 8. Total cost: 8 units. Preparation: 10–15 mins. Cooking: none.

Ingredients 8 oranges
200 g (7 oz) stoned dates
110 g (4 oz) whole almonds
100 ml (3 ½ fl oz) Bénédictine
1 soupspoon cinnamon
150 g (5 ½ oz) soft brown sugar

Method: Peel and slice the oranges finely. (Slice them on a plate to retain any juice). Chop the dates. Blanch and peel the almonds.

Dust the oranges with cinnamon and brown sugar. Arrange oranges, almonds and dates in individual compote dishes. Pour over any juice that may be on the plate.

Before serving pour a little Bénédictine over each portion.

Sorbet Belle de Mai
Sauternés Sorbet

Serves: 8. Total cost: 8 units. Preparation: 25–35 mins. Cooking: none. Other: freezing 24 hrs.

Ingredients 500 ml (17 fl oz) Sauternes
2 lemons
150 g (5 ½ oz) sugar
2 egg whites plus 30 g (1 oz) castor sugar

Method: Moisten the sugar with 150 ml (5 fl oz) water. Bring to the boil and simmer for 12 minutes until one has a well reduced syrup.

Zest the lemons. Infuse them in the syrup while it cools. Remove the zests. Stir in the juice of the lemons and the Sauternes. Beat the egg whites till stiff. Incorporate the castor sugar. Cook them over a bain-marie.

When the syrup is cold, fold in the meringue. Place in a freezer for 6 hours to bring the temperature right down. Now turn on the motor if you use an electric ice-cream machine. Otherwise leave till on the point of setting (it may take up to a day for the sorbet to set) and beat lightly to break down the crystals.

Note: Even with excellent equipment this is the hardest sorbet to make because of the high sugar content in the Sauternes and its alcohol content. With practice one realises when the sorbet is about to take and makes certain that the meringue is well mixed with the syrup until properly set.

Serve with early strawberries if possible.

Crêpes Fourrées au Chocolat
Chocolate Pancakes

Serves: 8. Total cost: 7 units. Preparation: 25–35 mins. Cooking: making the pancakes. Other: batter 1 hr.

Ingredients   *For 24 crêpes:*
250 g (9 oz) flour
3 eggs
500 ml (17 fl oz) milk
pinch of salt
50 g (scant 2 oz) butter
For the filling:
110 g (4 oz) plain chocolate
50 ml (1¾ fl oz) milk
2 yolks
50 g (scant 2 oz) castor sugar
60 g (2 oz) chopped candied lemon peel
2 soupspoons rum

Method: Mix flour, eggs, milk and salt. Let the batter stand for 1 hour. Make 24 pancakes.

Put milk and chocolate in a pan over a gentle heat. Cream the sugar and yolks. Add to the melted chocolate. Stir in rum. Mix in candied lemon peel.

Spread the chocolate filling over the pancakes and roll.

Note: To provide some variety one can make the filling with Curaçao and candied orange peel, giving a contrast of flavour.

Gratin de Rhubarbe
French Rhubarb Crumble

Serves: 8. Total cost: 6 units. Preparation: 25–30 mins. Cooking: 30 mins, plus 10 mins. Oven: 30 mins at 180°C/356°F/Gas Mk 4, 10 mins at 235°C/455°F/Gas Mk 8.

Ingredients   750 g (27 oz) rhubarb
200 g (7 oz) demerara sugar
For the crumble:
200 g (7 oz) self-raising flour
100 g (3½ oz) butter
For the crème:
60 g (2 oz) granulated sugar
30 g (1 oz) flour
3 eggs
200 ml (7 fl oz) milk
1 soupspoon Pernod

Method: Make a crème. Beat granulated sugar, egg yolks and flour. Pour over hot milk. Transfer to a clean pan. Bring to the boil stirring regularly. When thickened remove from heat and cool. Stiffly beat egg whites. Flavour the crème with Pernod. Fold in the whites.

Spread the crème in eight cassolettes (individual ovenproof dishes). Slice the rhubarb and arrange on the crème. Sprinkle with demerara sugar. Keep back one quarter of the demerara.

Crumb the butter and self-raising flour. Sprinkle over the fruit. Bake in a moderate oven 30 minutes.

Before serving, sprinkle remaining demerara sugar on the crumble. Place in a hot oven 10 minutes.

Note: This can be eaten either hot or cold.

Tarte au Citron

Lemon Tart

Serves: 8. Total cost: 5 units. Preparation: 30–40 mins. Cooking: lemon 6 mins, pastry 25 mins, meringue 10 mins. Other: resting paste 30 mins. Oven: pastry 190°C/374°F/Gas Mk 5, meringue 205°C/401°F/Gas Mk 6.

Ingredients   *For the pastry:*
280 g (10 oz) flour
20 g (scant 1 oz) ground almonds
grated zest of a lemon
150 g (5 ½ oz) butter
For the filling:
4 lemons
5 soupspoons Acacia honey
75 g (scant 3 oz) flour
3 yolks
For the meringue:
4 egg whites
60 g (2 oz) icing sugar
(butter and flour for lining tart ring)

Method: Sift the ground almond and flour. Add the grated zests. Crumb together with the butter. Moisten with a little water. Work into a ball and rest.

Butter and flour a tart ring. Roll out the paste and line. Bake blind in a moderate oven, about 25 minutes.

Grate the zests of three lemons. Infuse them in a cup of boiling water. Dissolve the flour in a bowl with the juice from the lemons and the water in which the zest infused. Pour the mixture into a pan. Bring to the boil, stirring with a wooden spoon. Cook out 5 or 6 minutes. If the sauce is too solid, lengthen with additional water. Stir in the honey. Take off the heat. Beat in the yolks. Spread the filling on the tart case. Cool.

Prepare the meringue. Stiffly beat the whites. Incorporate the icing sugar. Spoon over the lemon cream. Bake 10 minutes in a hot oven to cook the meringue.

Menu 5

First Courses

Main Courses

Sweets

First Courses

Maquereaux au Beaujolais
Mackerel with Beaujolais

Serves: 8. Total cost: 10 units. Preparation: 15–20 mins. Cooking: fish 6 mins, sauce 30 mins. Wine suggestion: Beaujolais.

Ingredients   8 small mackerel
grilling oil (page 32)
80 g (3 oz) butter
40 g (1 ½ oz) flour
1 bayleaf
1 small onion
1 piece smoked bacon rind
500 ml (17 fl oz) Beaujolais
salt and pepper

Method: Dice the onion. Fry in 50 g (1 ¾ oz) butter until it starts to brown.

Add the flour and cook out to a light brown roux. Pour the Beaujolais over the roux. Season with bayleaf and bacon rind. Simmer for at least 30 minutes.

Clean, wipe and season the mackerel. Brush with grilling oil. Grill about 6 minutes – depending on size.

Finish the sauce. Check seasoning. Pass the sauce through a chinois or sieve. Divide the rest of the butter into small knobs. Whisk into the sauce or use the liquidiser. Heat, but do not boil.

Serve the sauce separately from the mackerel.

Note: A common fault when making roux-based sauces in to make them too heavy. If the simmering reduces the sauce too quickly, lengthen with a little boiling water.

Soufflé d'Aubergines
Aubergine Soufflé

Serves: 8. Total cost: 8 units. Preparation: 35–45 mins. Cooking: 13 mins. Oven: 235°C/455°F/Gas Mk 8. Wine suggestion: Bordeaux – white Graves.

Ingredients   500 g (18 oz) aubergines
350 g (12 oz) tinned tomatoes
2 large onions
100 g (3½ oz) grated cheese (Parmesan for example)
1 teaspoon marjoram
1 teaspoon thyme
1 small chilli
5 large eggs and 1 white
100 ml (3½ fl oz) olive oil
100 ml (3½ fl oz) stiff béchamel sauce
salt
(butter and flour for the soufflé dishes)

Method: Peel and slice the aubergines. Chop the onions. Soften onions and aubergines in oil. Add the tomatoes and diced chilli. Season with salt and herbs. Stew for 15 minutes uncovered.

Add the grated cheese. Liquidise the aubergine mixture. Stir in the béchamel and egg yolks.

Beat the egg whites till stiff. Fold into the mixture.

Butter and flour eight individual soufflé dishes (see also Soufflé de Sole au Noilly, page 48). Pour mixture into each dish. Bake in a hot oven 13 minutes.

Note: This soufflé is extremely light and runs the risk of collapse in the time it takes to reach a customer's table. To counteract this *either* replace the béchamel with a roux (50 g (1¾ oz) flour plus 50 g (1¾ oz) butter) *or* add a teaspoon of baking powder to the béchamel before incorporating with the aubergine mixture. However, the author recommends the first method if possible.

Merlan Farci à la Toulonnaise
Whiting with Spinach and Curd Cheese

Serves: 8. Total cost: 11 units. Preparation: 20–30 mins. Cooking: 12 mins. Oven: 204°C/425°F/Gas Mk 7. Wine suggestion: Pouilly-Fumé.

Ingredients   8 whiting fillets
1 large onion
1 clove garlic
450 g (1 lb) spinach
110 g (4 oz) curd cheese

50 ml (1¾ fl oz) cream
nutmeg
200 g (7 oz) tomatoes
80 g (3 oz) butter
salt and pepper

Method: Blanch the spinach in boiling salted water. Drain. Liquidise and strain any excess moisture. Divide into two separate 'lots'.

Combine the first lot with curd cheese, nutmeg and seasoning. Combine the second lot with cream, nutmeg and seasoning. Spread the cheese and spinach mixture over the skin-side of the fillets. Fold the fillets around the mixture.

Butter a gratin dish. Cover with a layer of the spinach and cream mixture. Arrange the whiting fillets on the bed of spinach. Brush with melted butter.

Blanch, skin and pip the tomatoes. Dice the tomatoes, onion and garlic, and sweat in butter. Pour the mixture over the fillets. Bake in a hot oven 12 minutes.

Note: A little sorrel, if one can obtain it, mixed with the spinach is an improvement.

Pâté de Canard aux Pistaches
Duck Pâté with Pistachio Nuts

Serves: 8. Total cost: 13 units. Preparation: 40–50 mins. Cooking: 1½ hrs. Other: macerating the meats 6 hrs. Oven: 15 mins at 235°C/455°F/Gas Mk 8, 1¼ hrs at 175°C/347°F/Gas Mk 4. Wine suggestion: Hermitage rouge.

Ingredients   1 2kg (4½ lb) duck
450 g (1 lb) belly of pork
30 g (1 oz) pistachios
2 shallots
1 soupspoon cognac
1 egg
25 ml (¾ fl oz) double cream
1 teaspoon thyme
salt and pepper
For the croûte:
350 g (12 oz) flour
200 g (7 oz) butter
1 large egg
1 yolk
(butter for lining the dish)

Method: Chop the duck meat. Mince the liver and belly of pork. Dice the shallots. Mix together these ingredients with cognac, lightly beaten egg, cream, thyme, salt and pepper. Leave half a day.

Prepare a rich shortcrust pastry. Crumb flour and butter. Beat in egg. Butter a raised pie dish. Line the dish with two-thirds of the paste. Spread a layer of farce on the paste. Sprinkle with pistachios. Cover with the remainder of the farce. Roll out the rest of the paste. Water the edges and seal over the pâté. Make a chimney with scraps of paste. Cut out a hole in the pastry lid. Fix the chimney above it. Brush the lid with egg yolk.

Bake 15 minutes in a hot oven. Turn down the heat to moderate. Continue baking for a further 1¼ hours.

Note: Rather than waste the duck fat, place the skin in a pan and render down. Allow to set. There should be enough to use as shortening in place of butter when making the 'croûte'. This will also improve the duck's flavour.

Salade Chinoise
Mixed Salad with Bean Sprouts

Serves: 8. Total cost: 9 units. Preparation: 15–25 mins. Cooking: none. Wine suggestion: Moselle.

Ingredients   220 g (8 oz) bean sprouts
140 g (5 oz) mushrooms
1 large grapefruit
2 shallots
1 avocado pear
1 lemon
350 g (12 oz) pickled ox tongue
soya sauce
salt and pepper

Method: Wipe and slice the mushrooms. Moisten with lemon juice to prevent them discolouring. Wash and drain the bean sprouts. Peel and cube the grapefruit. Finely dice the shallots. Dice the tongue into strips.

Peel the avocado pear. Remove the stone. Slice into strips. Moisten with lemon juice.

Toss all the ingredients together in salad bowl. Season with soya sauce, salt and pepper.

Salade 'à ma Façon'
Chicken and Mayonnaise Salad

Serves: 8. Total cost: 13 units. Preparation: 20–30 mins. Cooking: none. Other: poaching the chicken 1 hr. Wine suggestion: Chablis.

Ingredients
1 small, boiled chicken
1 celery heart
celery leaves
220 g (8 oz) mushrooms
1 soupspoon chopped tarragon
small pinch of saffron
200 ml (7 fl oz) mayonnaise
½ lemon

Method: Boil the chicken using the outer stalks of celery in the bouillon, besides the usual carrot, onion, bouquet garni.

Remove skin. Cube meat, keeping leg and breast separate.

Slice the mushrooms and brush with oil. Chop the celery into bâtons (strips a little wider than a fine julienne).

Work the saffron, the lemon juice and half the tarragon into the mayonnaise.

Arrange the leg-meat on individual dishes.

Combine mushroom, celery and breast-meat in the mayonnaise. Spoon the mixture on top of the leg-meat. Garnish with the rest of the tarragon and celery leaves.

Champignons Farcis
Mushroom Heads Stuffed with Chicken Liver

Serves: 8. Total cost: 6 units. Preparation: 25–35 mins. Cooking: included in preparation. Wine suggestion: Moselle.

Ingredients	32 large button mushrooms	80 g (3 oz) butter
	6 chicken livers	1 teaspoon tarragon
	400 g (14 oz) tinned tomatoes	50 g (scant 2 oz) white
	1 lemon	breadcrumbs
	6 shallots	salt and pepper

Method: Remove the stalks of the mushrooms. Sweat the heads in 50 g (scant 2 oz) butter and the juice of a lemon. Season.

Rinse the chicken livers under a cold tap. Dice the shallots and mushroom stalks.

Drain the mushroom heads and keep warm. Sweat the mushroom stalks and shallots in the same pan as the heads. Add the tomatoes and reduce to a thick consistency. Dice the livers and add to the pan together with tarragon. Season.

Spread the mixture on each mushroom head. Sprinkle with seasoned breadcrumbs. Dot with remaining butter. Place under a grill/salamander to gratinate.

Pissaladière
Tomato, Anchovy and Olive Tart

Serves: 8. Total cost: 6 units. Preparation: 25–35 mins. Cooking: pastry 25 mins, filling 20 mins. Other: resting paste 30 mins. Oven: 190°C/374°F/Gas Mk 5. Wine suggestion: Rosé de Provence.

Ingredients   *For the pastry:*
350 g (12 oz) flour
200 g (7 oz) butter
2 eggs
(butter and flour for tart ring)
For the coulis:
600 g (21 oz) tinned tomatoes
200 g (7 oz) aubergines
200 g (7 oz) onions
50 ml (1¾ fl oz) olive oil
15 fresh basil leaves
1 teaspoon oregano
salt and pepper
For the garnish:
8 black olives
8 anchovy fillets

Method: Prepare a shortcrust pastry. Crumb flour and butter. Beat in whole eggs. Roll into a ball. Rest.

Butter and flour a tart ring. Line with rolled out paste. Bake blind, 25 minutes in a moderate oven.

155

Bistro Style Cookery

Peel and chop the aubergines. Peel and chop the onion. Sweat till tender in the olive oil. Add the tomatoes. Simmer till any excess moisture has evaporated. Cool.

Place the 'ratatouille' in a liquidiser with basil and oregano. Blend. Check seasoning.

Spread the coulis over the pastry. Garnish with olives and anchovy fillets.

Main Courses

157

Potée au Pistou
Boiled Hock with Basil and Garlic

Serves: 8. Total cost: 20 units. Preparation: 20–30 mins. Cooking: 2 hrs 20 mins. Other: soaking the hock and haricot beans 12 hrs. Wine suggestion: Bandol.

Ingredients   1 hock (about 2 kg, 4 ½ –5 lb)
6 carrots
6 turnips
450 g (1 lb) tomatoes
12 small courgettes
150 g (5 ½ oz) French beans
150 (5 ½ oz) haricot beans
250 g (9 oz) peas or mange-tout
1 saucisson or a 250 g (9 oz) piece of chorizo
For the pistou:
15 basil leaves
4 cloves of garlic
3 soupspoons olive oil
For the garnish:
150 g (5 ½ oz) Parmesan

Method: Soak the hock overnight. Soak the haricot beans.

Place the hock in a large pan. Cover with cold water. Bring to the boil and simmer for 1 hour.

Slice the carrots. Chop turnips coarsely. Add carrots, turnips, skinned tomatoes, haricot beans and the saucisson to the stock. Simmer for a second hour.

Add French beans, peas and coarsely-chopped courgettes to the stock. Simmer 20 minutes more.

Prepare the pistou. Liquidise basil, olive oil and garlic. Whisk a little stock on to the pistou and then mix with the rest of the stock and the vegetables.

Slice the hock and serve on a separate dish. Serve with Parmesan cheese.

Note: One needs a large appetite to eat a first course before this dish!

Côtelettes à la Soubise
Glazed Lamb Cutlets with Onion Purée

Serves: 8. Total cost: 21 units. Preparation: 30–40 mins. Cooking: soubise 35 mins, lamb 6–8 mins, sauce 15 mins. Wine suggestion: Châteauneuf du Pape.

Ingredients   16 loin chops
2 litres (3½ pints) chicken stock
salt and pepper
For the soubise:
4 large onions
200 ml (7 fl oz) stiff béchamel
80 g (3 oz) butter
8 juniper berries
nutmeg
50 ml (1¾ fl oz) cream
salt and pepper

Method: Prepare the soubise. Slice the onions. Blanch 5 minutes in boiling, salted water. Drain. Sweat till tender, without colouring, in butter.

Add crushed juniper berries, nutmeg and béchamel to pan. Cover. Stew in a moderate oven 30 minutes.

Pour in cream. Liquidise. Check seasoning.

Trim the cutlets. Place trimmings in a sauteuse with unseasoned stock. Reduce rapidly.

Grill the cutlets, 3 minutes on each side.

When the stock has reduced almost to a glaze, season and add the cutlets to the pan. Leave just long enough to glaze, 2 minutes at the most.

Serve the cutlets on a bed of soubise. Spoon any surplus glaze over them.

Note: There are several different recipes for soubise. This one should be a cross between a purée and a sauce.

Bar Braisé aux Aromates
Bass Braised with Marjoram, Mint and Vegetables

Serves: 8. Total cost: 21 units. Preparation: 15–25 mins. Cooking: about 12 mins. Wine suggestion: Bourgogne Aligoté.

Ingredients   8 escalopes of bass (taken from 1 large bass)
200 g (7 oz) onion
100 g (3 ½ oz) pimentoes   1 soupspoon marjoram
100 g (3 ½ oz) cucumber   1 soupspoon mint
100 g (3 ½ oz) celery   80 g (3 oz) butter
50 g (scant 2 oz) fennel   200 ml (7 fl oz) fish stock
2 cloves garlic   salt and pepper

Method: Finely dice all the vegetables and garlic. Sweat them in the butter 10 minutes. Add the stock. Season. Place the fish on a bed of vegetables. Garnish with chopped herbs. Cover. Braise until the fish is cooked.

Baste the escalopes with the stock. (If using the fish whole turn after 12 minutes and braise for a further 6 minutes.)

Note: Resist the temptation to add other herbs to those mentioned; they would destroy the balance of the dish. Equally, there is no need to serve a sauce as an accompaniment.

Poitrine de Veau aux Oignons Blancs
Breast of Veal with Spring Onions

Serves: 8. Total cost: 18 units. Preparation: 25–35 mins. Cooking: 50 mins. Wine suggestion: Bordeaux – St Julien.

Ingredients   1600 g (58 oz) breast of veal
2 onions
250 g (9 oz) mushrooms
80 g (3 oz) butter
50 g (scant 2 oz) flour
1 soupspoon cognac
1 ½ litres (52 fl oz) veal stock
750 g (about 26 oz) spring onions
150 ml (5 fl oz) cream
salt and pepper

L

Method: Trim the meat taking care that all the sinews have been removed. Cut into domino-sized pieces. Sauté in the butter till well coloured. Deglaze the pan with cognac. Flame. Stir in flour.

Chop onions and mushrooms. Return veal to pan with onions and mushrooms. Pour over stock. Simmer covered for 30 minutes.

Trim and clean the spring onions. Add them to pan. Reduce sauce slowly so that the meat will have time to finish cooking (about 50 minutes altogether).

Stir in cream. Check seasoning.

Aiglefin à la Basquaise
Haddock with Peppers, Onions and Tomatoes

Serves: 8. Total cost: 16 units. Preparation: 20–25 mins. Cooking: garnish 25 mins, fish 12–15 mins. Wine suggestion: white Rioja – Marquis de Murrieta.

Ingredients
8 haddock fillets
1 large onion
2 red peppers
2 large green peppers
50 g (scant 2 oz) tomato purée
600 g (21 oz) tinned tomatoes
2 cloves garlic
1 teaspoon soft brown sugar
1 bayleaf
1 teaspoon thyme
1 teaspoon chopped parsley
100 ml (3½ fl oz) olive oil
salt and pepper

Method: Dice the onion. Fry in olive oil till it starts to brown. Add chopped garlic. Add peppers, peeled and cut into fine julienne strips. Stew gently for 10 minutes.

Stir the tomato purée, tomatoes, herbs and sugar into the pepper mixture. Simmer uncovered for 15 minutes more. Check seasoning.

Arrange fillets on this bed of vegetables. Cover pan and braise until the haddock is cooked.

Note: Bearing in mind the middle-class 'fish-snobbery' which turns up its nose at anything but sole, trout and shellfish, a restaurant might be advised to substitute the haddock with sautéd chicken.

Poussin Poêlé en Cocotte au Fenouil
Young Chicken Stewed with Butter and Fennel

Serves: 8. Total cost: 28 units. Preparation: 15–20 mins. Cooking: 20 mins. Oven: 235°C/455°F/Gas Mk 8. Wine suggestion: Beaujolais – Juliénas.

Ingredients   8 poussins   500 g (18 oz) butter
1 kg (2¼ lb) fennel   100 ml (3½ fl oz) cream
350 g (12 oz) celery   fennel leaves
350 g (12 oz) onions   salt and pepper

Method: Slice the fennel, dice the celery and onion. Blanch 5 minutes in boiling water.

Rub the poussins with butter. Season them.

Butter a large cocotte (ovenproof dish). Place the fennel in first. Place the poussins on top of the fennel. Bake covered in a very hot oven for 20 minutes. Combine cream with vegetables.

Garnish with chopped fennel leaves.

Note: To prepare the fennel, trim top stalks keeping any leaves for garnishing, peel the fibrous outside leaves, quarter the bulb and slice as finely as possible.

Médaillons d'Agneau au Madère
Medallions of Lamb with a Madeira Sauce

Serves: 8. Total cost: 20 units. Preparation: 40–50 mins. Cooking: medallions 2 mins, kidneys about 2 mins. Wine suggestion: Bordeaux – St Estèphe.

Ingredients   1½ kg (48 oz) best end of lamb
80 g (3 oz) butter
salt and pepper
For the croûtons:
8 slices white bread
100 g (3½ oz) butter
For the sauce:
400 ml (14 fl oz) Madeira sauce (see page 41)
2 lambs' kidneys
50 g (scant 2 oz) butter

163

Method: Bone the best end of lamb. Trim any flank except for 2½ cm (1 in) of fat next to the eye.

On the slant, slice the eye of meat into medallions. Flatten each one lightly with a cutlet bat. Trim the attached fat so it forms a triangle at the end of each piece.

Trim the crusts of the bread. Slice across the diagonal. Shape into hearts. Fry in butter.

Slice the kidneys. Sauté lightly in butter. Drain and wipe with kitchen paper. Heat the Madeira sauce. Before serving add the sliced kidneys.

Fry the medallions of lamb a minute on each side only so that the flesh inside is still pink. Adjust seasoning.

Arrange on croûtons. Coat with the Madeira sauce.

Daube Béarnaise

Beef Simmered in a sealed pot with Smoked Bacon

Serves: 8. Total cost: 21 units. Preparation: 15–20 mins. Cooking: 4 hrs. Oven: 160°C/320°F/Gas Mk 2. Wine suggestion: Corbières.

Ingredients	
	1400 g (50 oz) topside
	2 onions
	4 carrots
	300 g (11 oz) lean smoked bacon
	200 g (7 oz) mushrooms
	150 ml (5 fl oz) red wine
	salt and pepper
	(flour and water)

Method: Cut the topside into eight 'steaks' or leave tied in a single piece. Dice bacon. Place meats on a bed of the roughly chopped vegetables. Moisten with wine. Cover with water. Season (only a little salt because of the bacon). Seal the lid with a flour and water paste. Simmer in a low oven for 4 hours.

Note: This dish takes its name from Béarn, so one ought to use Jambon de Bayonne instead of lean smoked bacon.

As far as the recipe goes it seems closer to a 'plat familial' than a restaurant dish. To give it a little more distinction, allow the daube to cool. Skim off the surface fat. Braise shredded cabbage (red or white) in the fat. Re-heat the daube. Add a few potatoes to it and simmer till they are tender. Serve the topside on the cabbage surrounded by vegetables with a sauceboat for the cooking juices.

Steak Madrague
Entrecôte Steak with a Garlic Dressing

Serves: 8. Total cost: 32 units. Preparation: 10–15 mins. Cooking: 5–12 mins. Wine suggestion: Bordeaux – St Julien.

Ingredients   8 × 200 g (7 oz) entrecôte steaks
3 cloves garlic
3 spring onions
2 soupspoons tarragon vinegar
1 soupspoon chopped parsley
130 g (4 ½ oz) unsalted butter
salt and pepper
(grilling oil, page 32)

Method: Oil the steaks. Grill them as required (5–12 minutes).

Finely dice the spring onions and garlic. Sauté in 100 g (3 ½ oz) butter till golden. Add the tarragon vinegar and chopped parsley to the pan. Season with salt and pepper.

Off the heat, whisk the rest of the butter (softened) into the sauce. Spoon a little of the mixture over each steak.

Sweets

Le Milliard

Black Cherries Baked in Batter

Serves: 8. Total cost: 8 units. Preparation: 15 mins. Cooking: 30 mins. Other: batter 1 hr. Oven: 200°C/392°F/Gas Mk 6.

Ingredients   4 eggs
100 g (3½ oz) flour
50 g (scant 2 oz) liquid honey
450 ml (16 fl oz) milk
700 g (25 oz) black cherries
20 g (scant 1 oz) butter
(icing sugar)

Method: Prepare a batter. Beat together flour, honey, milk and eggs. Rest for 1 hour.

Butter a large porcelain flan dish. Pour the batter into the flan dish. Garnish with cherries. Bake in a moderately hot oven for 30 minutes.

Serve either hot or cold with clotted cream. If cold one may garnish with icing sugar.

Note: Le Milliard is a type of clafoutis. It takes its name from a variety of cherry grown in Auvergne. Morello cherries, which are available in this country, are an acceptable substitute. In fact one may vary the flavour with the cherry. Honey can be replaced with sugar but is more indigestible, an important factor in a restaurant where most meals are eaten before customers go to bed.

Petits Pâtés de Groseilles à Maquereau

Gooseberry Tartlets

Serves: 8. Total cost: 4 units. Preparation: 30 mins. Cooking: 1 hr. Oven: 165°C/329°F/Gas Mk 3.

Ingredients   650 g (1lb 7 oz) gooseberries
220 (8 oz) demerara sugar   2 yolks
(elder flowers optional)   200 ml (7 fl oz) water
400 g (14 oz) flour   150 g (5½ oz) butter
large pinch of salt   (groundnut oil)

167

Method: Place the flour in a bowl with the salt. Add the yolks and cover with flour.

Boil the butter and water. Beat the liquid into the flour. Mix to a smooth paste. Rest in the kitchen 15 minutes (not in fridge).

Oil 8 ramekin dishes. Divide the pastry into 8 pieces. Divide each piece into two (one for lining the ramekin, one for the lid). Roll the pastry finely. Line the ramekins. Fill each one with gooseberries (adding elder flowers if wished) and plenty of demerara sugar. Retain a little sugar for finishing. Cover the gooseberries with pastry lids, carefully sealing the edges. Sprinkle with remaining sugar.

Place the ramekins in a bain-marie, in a low oven. After 30 minutes, take them out of the bain-marie and bake normally for another 30 minutes. Cool. Turn out the little pies on to a dish. Chill. Serve with cream.

Note: Turning out the pies demands care. Place the ramekins on their sides. Lift slightly and tap the bottoms. The pies will fall out on to the plate. Stand them upright before chilling.

Diplomate de Framboises
Raspberry Diplomat

Serves: 8. Total cost: 15 units. Preparation: 25–35 mins. Cooking: 15 mins. Other: setting 24 hrs. Oven: 220°C/428°F/Gas Mk 7.

Ingredients *For the biscuits:*
160 g (5½ oz) castor sugar
4 eggs
115 g (4 oz) flour
vanilla essence
icing sugar
(butter)
For the filling and garnish:
5 macaroons
450 g (1 lb) raspberries
1 pot Tiptree raspberry jam
1 soupspoon kirsch

Method: Make the biscuits. Beat the sugar and yolks to the ribbon. Add the vanilla essence. Stir in the flour. Beat the whites till stiff. Fold into the mixture. Fill a piping bag plus medium size plain tube with the mixture. Butter sheets of grease-proof paper on baking trays. Pipe 8 cm (3 in) fingers (about 40) of paste 4 cm (1 ½ in) apart on the trays, the mixture is right if it holds its shape without spreading. Dredge with icing sugar. Bake the biscuits à la cuillère (sponge fingers) in a hot oven 15 minutes.

Dilute the kirsch with 150 ml (5 fl oz) water. Dip the biscuits one by one in the mixture. Arrange a layer of biscuits on the bottom of a charlotte mould. Spread with raspberry jam.

Crush the macaroons. Sprinkle some of the crushed macaroons over the jam. Follow with a handful of raspberries. Continue with layers of biscuits, jam, macaroon and raspberries till the mould is filled. Finish with a layer of biscuits. Weight the mould with a dish. Chill. Turn out. Garnish with remaining raspberries.

Note: To avoid any risk of sticking, place a ring of greaseproof paper on the bottom of the mould before placing the first layer of biscuits.

Hazelnut Meringue Gâteau with Strawberries

Serves: 8. Total cost: 10 units. Preparation: 25–35 mins. Cooking: meringues 2–3 hrs. Oven: 15 mins at 180°C/356°F/Gas Mk 4, about 2½ hrs at 90°C/194°F/Gas Mk ¼.

Ingredients   500 g (18 oz) strawberries
300 ml (10 fl oz) cream
50 g (scant 2 oz) castor sugar
1 soupspoon kirsch
(butter and flour)
For the meringue:
4 egg whites
220 g (8 oz) castor sugar
150 g (5 ½ oz) roasted hazelnuts

Method: Chop the hazelnuts finely, but not so much that they are ground.

Make a meringue with the whites and sugar. Beat the whites adding three-quarters of the sugar gradually. When quite stiff and glossy, add the rest of the sugar and whisk for 3 minutes more. Fold in the hazelnuts.

Butter and flour two rings of greaseproof paper. Pipe meringue rings on the paper. Place in a moderate oven till the meringues begin to colour. Turn the oven right down and allow to dry out.

Beat the cream with sugar and kirsch. Spread a layer of cream on a meringue ring. Garnish with halved strawberries. Spread cream on the underside of the second meringue. Place on top of the strawberries.

Garnish with the remaining cream and a few strawberries kept back for the purpose.

Summer Pudding

Serves: 8. Total cost: 10 units. Preparation: 15–20 mins. Cooking: 15 mins. Other: setting the pudding 24 hrs.

Ingredients 1 kg (36 oz) blackcurrants
450 g (1 lb) eating apples
220 g (8 oz) sugar
1 loaf of white bread

Method: Peel and quarter the apples. Poach the apples and blackcurrants with sugar and 75 ml (about 2½ fl oz) water for 15 minutes. Strain the fruit and reserve. Keep the juice.

Cut the crusts from a loaf of white bread (preferably not too fresh). Slice the loaf, roughly the thickness of a piece of toast. Cut each slice into three lengthwise. Dip the bread, a piece at a time into the blackcurrant juice. Line the base and sides of a charlotte mould with the bread. Fill the mould with the blackcurrants and apples. Cover with a layer of bread. Weight the pudding. Place overnight in a fridge.

Turn out. Serve with clotted cream.

Note: One may use most varieties of soft fruit to make a summer pudding. Blackcurrants are best, though. The apple is there to hold the pudding together.

Pêches au Fino

Peaches with Fino Sherry

Serves: 8. Total cost: 7 units. Preparation: 10–15 mins. Cooking: 40 mins. Other: chilling the peaches. Oven: 160°C/320°F/Gas Mk 2.

Ingredients   8 large peaches
2 oranges
150 g (5 ½ oz) sugar
250 ml (7 fl oz) Fino sherry

Method: Blanch the peaches in boiling water for 2 minutes. Peel. Place them in an ovenproof dish. Add the sugar. Scrub two oranges to remove chemical traces in the skin. Finely slice them. Add to the peaches. Pour over 150 ml (5 fl oz) Fino and enough water to cover. Bring to the boil. Bake in a warm oven for 40 minutes. Cool.

Put the peaches into individual serving dishes with slices of orange and their cooking liquor. Leave in the freezer until the juice is on the point of turning into ice. Pour the remainder of Fino (chilled) over each peach. Serve.

Menu 6

August–September

First Courses
page 175

Main Courses
page 184

Sweets
page 193

First Courses

Maquereaux Marinés à la Crème de Noix
Mackerel Fillets in Walnut Cream

Serves: 8. Total cost: 8 units. Preparation: 20–30 mins. Cooking: none. Other: marinading 48 hrs. Wine suggestion: Sauvignon.

Ingredients   4 large mackerel
1 onion
500 ml (17 fl oz) wine vinegar
1 soupspoon sugar
1 teaspoon allspice
2 soupspoons chopped dill
1 teaspoon green peppercorns
sea salt

Method: Fillet the mackerel.

Prepare a marinade. Chop the onion. Mix together with other ingredients in a shallow container.

Lay the fillets, skin upward in the marinade. Add enough water to cover. Leave for about 2 days until the vinegar has 'cooked' the mackerel.

Walnut Cream

Ingredients   200 ml (7 fl oz) cream
100 g (3 ½ oz) walnuts
1 lemon
salt and pepper

Method: Whisk the cream till stiff. Incorporate the grated zest and juice of lemon to taste. Season.

Coarsely chop the walnuts. Fold into the cream.

Bisque de Crabe
Crab Bisque

Serves: 8. Total cost: 8 units. Preparation: 20–30 mins. Cooking: 20 mins. Wine suggestion: Muscadet.

Ingredients 220 g (8 oz) crab meat
1 onion
2 carrots
3 tomatoes
300 ml (10 fl oz) white wine
100 g (3½ oz) butter
50 g (scant 2 oz) flour
1 heaped teaspoon paprika
1 yolk
2 soupspoons cream
salt and cayenne pepper

Method: Fry the finely diced carrot and onion in half the butter. When they start to colour, add the quartered tomatoes. Stew 5 minutes. Moisten with wine and add 1½ litres (about 2½ pints) water. Bring to the boil. Add the crab meat. Simmer 20 minutes. Liquidise. Pass through a fine sieve.

Make a roux with the remaining butter and flour. Pour the liquidised soup on to the roux. Season with salt, paprika and a small pinch of cayenne. Simmer 15 minutes.

Prepare a liaison of cream and yolks. Whisk the bisque on to the liaison. Serve.

Terrine de Poisson à la Sauce Verte
Fish Terrine with a Herb Sauce

Serves: 8. Total cost: 10 units. Preparation: 25–35 mins. Cooking: 1¼ hrs. Other: cooling 1 hr. Oven: 180°C/356°F/Gas Mk 4. Wine suggestion: Corton blanc.

Ingredients 2 large lemon soles
450 g (1 lb) whiting
3 egg whites
3 slices bread soaked in milk and squeezed
200 ml (7 fl oz) double cream
1 soupspoon tomato purée
1 teaspoon nutmeg

1 soupspoon chopped chives
1 teaspoon chopped dill
200 g (7 oz) onions
200 g (7 oz) mushrooms
50 g (scant 2 oz) butter
4 large pancakes
salt and pepper

Method: Skin and fillet the soles.

Dice the onion and mushrooms. Sweat in butter.

Fillet the whiting. Blend the fish to a purée (as for quenelles). Season with salt, pepper, nutmeg, chives and dill. Mix in tomato purée. Add bread to the fish purée and blend well. Repeat with the egg whites. Place in the fridge for 1 hour.

Add the cream straight from the fridge. Blend. The mixture will resemble a quenelle mix.

Oil a rectangular terrine. Arrange the pancakes so they line the terrine. Mix a quarter of the fish purée with the onion/mushroom duxelles. Spread half the remaining purée over the pancake at the base of the terrine. Cover with seasoned sole fillets. Now spread the duxelles/purée mixture on the fillets. Cover with the rest of the fillets. Finish with a layer of the fish purée.

Fold flaps of pancake to cover the fish. Cover with foil. Bake in a bain-marie, in a moderate oven 1¼ hours.

Fig 1.   Cross section of terrine
(a) Purée
(b) Sole
(c) Duxelles
(d) Pancake

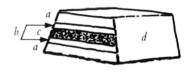

Sauce Verte

Ingredients   20 g (⅔ oz) sorrel
150 ml (5 fl oz) mayonnaise
1 lemon

Method: Liquidise the sorrel with lemon juice and beat into mayonnaise while adding the oil.

Note: There are many different versions of this mayonnaise-based sauce. This one is most suited to the terrine.

Crudités
Mixed Vegetables Salads

Serves: 8. Total cost: 10 units. Preparation: 45–60 mins (total for 5 dishes). Cooking: beans 7–10 mins, potatoes 20 mins. Other: to dégorger the cucumber 1 hr. Wine suggestion: Moselle.

Haricots Verts

Ingredients   250 g (9 oz) haricots verts (French beans)
2 large cloves garlic
1 soupspoon chopped parsley
chervil (if available)
2 soupspoons wine vinegar
6 soupspoons groundnut oil
salt and pepper

Method: Boil the beans in salted water for 7 to 10 minutes depending on how fine they are.

Prepare a vinaigrette with oil, vinegar, crushed garlic, parsley, chervil (if available), salt and pepper. Just before serving toss the beans in the vinaigrette.

Fennel and Orange

Ingredients   1 large bulb of fennel
2 oranges – preferably blood oranges
salt and pepper

Method: Trim the stalks of the fennel. Peel outer skin (Note page 163). Slice finely. Peel and slice oranges on a porcelain dish. Combine fennel and oranges. Season. Pour any juice on the dish over the salad.

Tomato and Black Olive

Ingredients   450 g (1 lb) tomatoes
100 g (3½ oz) black olives
50 ml (1¾ fl oz) unprocessed olive oil (preferably unblended)
salt and pepper

Method: Wash the olives. Wipe. Shake them in olive oil. Blanch and peel the tomatoes. Quarter or slice to taste. Season. Toss in olive oil. Garnish with black olives.

Cucumber and Yoghurt

Ingredients   1 cucumber   1 small pot yoghurt
sea salt   salt and pepper
1 sprig mint   paprika

Method: Peel, core and slice the cucumber. Place in a colander. Sprinkle with sea salt. Allow to dégorger for an hour. Rinse thoroughly. Wipe.

179

Chop the mint. Combine mint, yoghurt and seasoning. Arrange cucumber on a dish. Spoon the yoghurt dressing over it. Garnish with a little paprika.

New Potatoes

Ingredients   450 g (1 lb) new potatoes
3 shallots
1 soupspoon Dijon mustard
1 ½ soupspoons wine vinegar
6 soupspoons groundnut oil

Method: Boil the new potatoes in their skins. Cool. Quarter.

Dice the shallots. Slightly heat the Dijon mustard and vinegar. Add shallots, oil and seasoning. Combine warm vinaigrette with potatoes just before serving.

Note: The author excuses himself for stretching the meaning of 'crudités'.

Oeufs en Cocotte à l'Estragon

Baked Eggs with Cream and Tarragon

Serves: 8. Total cost: 6 units. Preparation: 15–20 mins. Cooking: 8 mins. Oven: 235°C/455°F/Gas Mk 8. Wine suggestion: Sylvaner.

Ingredients   8 eggs
8 chicken livers
80 g (3 oz) butter
100 g (3 ½ oz) mushrooms
80 g (3 oz) onions
1 teaspoon cognac
1 soupspoon tarragon
8 soupspoons cream
salt and pepper

Method: Dice the onion and mushrooms. Sauté in 50 g (1 ¾ oz) butter. Add the rest of the butter. Sauté the livers with the duxelles. Deglaze with cognac. season.

Spoon liver and duxelles into eight cassolettes. Break an egg into each dish. Spoon cream over the egg. Bake the eggs 8 minutes in a hot oven. Garnish with tarragon.

Gogues
Slices of a Spinach, Lettuce and Pork Sausage

Serves: 8. Total cost: 8 units. Preparation: 25–35 mins. Cooking: (i) 2 hrs, (ii) 8 mins. Other: salting greens 12 hrs. Wine suggestion: Loire – Sancerre.

Ingredients   200 g (7 oz) spinach
200 g (7 oz) lettuce
200 g (7 oz) onion
80 g (3 oz) lard
300 g (10½ oz) belly of pork
300 g (10½ oz) streaky bacon
80 g (3 oz) pig's liver
1 egg
1 level teaspoon nutmeg
1 level teaspoon allspice
1 soupspoon chopped tarragon
sausage skins
salt and pepper

Method: Finely chop the spinach, onion and lettuce. Salt and leave overnight.

Dice the belly of pork and the bacon. Soften in half the lard for 30 minutes. Drain. Add the remaining lard to the pan. Stew the lettuce, onion and spinach in the lard till tender, about 20 minutes. Mix them together with the lard, belly of pork and bacon mixture. Blend the mixture in the liquidiser adding raw liver, nutmeg, allspice, tarragon, egg, salt and pepper.

Feed this forcemeat into the sausage skins. Bear in mind that the egg will cause the skins to stretch during poaching. The forcemeat should make about 10 sausages. Poach these in hardly boiling salted water for 2 hours. Cool.

Slice the cooked sausages into discs, five or six per portion. Brush with butter and lightly fry till they start to colour. Serve, perhaps with some Béarnaise sauce.

Galantine de Volaille
Chicken Galantine

**Serves: 10. Total cost: 10 units. Preparation: 35–45 mins.
Cooking: 3 hrs. Other: soaking chicken skin 2 hrs. Wine
suggestion: Pinot-Chardonnay.**

Ingredients 1 medium chicken
200 g (7 oz) stewing veal
1 onion
100 ml (3½ fl oz) cream
1 egg (or 2 yolks)
nutmeg
1 soupspoon chopped tarragon
salt and pepper
For the stock:
1 litre (1¾ pints) chicken stock
200 ml (7 fl oz) white wine
2 branches tarragon
salt and pepper

Method: Bone the chicken (see Galantine page 39). Soak the skin in
cold water for 2 hours.

Combine the veal, the onion and all the chicken meat, bar 1 breast. Put
twice through the mincer. Lightly beat the egg. Work the egg, tarragon,
nutmeg, cream and seasoning into the farce.

Spread the skin on the preparation surface. Spread half the quantity of
farce on the centre area of skin.

Slice the breast that has been kept back into strips. Arrange these strips
on the farce. Cover with the remainder of the farce. Wrap the edges of
skin over the farce. Fasten them with a cocktail stick. Roll the galantine
into a cylindrical shape. Wrap in a clean cloth. Tie both ends of cloth
with kitchen string.

Chop the chicken carcass, bones, neck and giblets. Place them in a pan.
Place the galantine on top. Pour over the stock, white wine and enough
water to cover the galantine. Add the tarragon. Season. Bring to the
boil. Skim off any impurities. Simmer 3 hours, covered. Drain the
galantine. Cool.

Note: Once the stock has cooled it may set to a jelly. A little jelly
chopped into cubes can accompany the galantine. If not reduce the
liquid by half which will almost certainly be sufficient to set the stock.

Crème Cressonnière
Cream of Watercress Soup

Serves: 8. Total cost: 6 units. Preparation: 10–15 mins. Cooking: 5 mins. Wine suggestion: in accordance with the main course.

Ingredients   3 bunches watercress
80 g (3 oz) butter
60 g (2 oz) flour
1 large onion
nutmeg
500 ml (17 fl oz) milk
600 ml (1 pint) chicken stock
150 ml (5 fl oz) cream
salt and pepper

Method: Chop the watercress finely.

Dice the onion. Sweat in the butter till transparent. Stir in flour. Add the cress. Pour over the milk and stock. Bring to the boil. Simmer 5 minutes. Cool. Liquidise. Season with salt, pepper and nutmeg. Re-heat. Finish with cream.

Note: The thing to avoid is overcooking the cress. It will turn grey if simmered too long and lose both its colour and its fresh flavour. Covering the soup may also turn it prematurely grey!

Main Courses

Poisson à la Tahitienne
Marinaded Hake Salad with Coconut Milk

Serves: 8. Total cost: 14 units. Preparation: 35–45 mins. Other: marinading the fish 2 hrs. Wine suggestion: Pouilly-Fuissé.

Ingredients

1100 g (2⅓ lb) hake	3 tomatoes
1 coconut	3 hard-boiled eggs
3 lemons	2 cloves garlic
3 grapefruit	2 peppers (1 green and 1 red)
1 onion	1 soupspoon tarragon
1 bunch spring onions	salt and pepper

Method: Skin and fillet the hake. Soak in salted water for 8 minutes. Wash. Dice into mouthful-sized cubes. Squeeze the juice of the lemons and the grapefruit. Marinade the cubes of fish for 2 hours, turning over at regular intervals.

Split the coconut. Blend or grate the meat. Squeeze the coconut meat through a cloth to extract the milk. Reserve the milk. Mix with tarragon and crushed garlic.

Prepare individual salad bowls with julienne of peppers, spring onions and onion rings, hard-boiled eggs and tomatoes. Season.

Drain the fish, which should be perfectly white. Arrange on the bed of salad. Pour the coconut milk over the fish and salad as a dressing.

Note: Under no circumstances use any but 'wet' fish for this dish. The fresher the fish, the less it needs to marinade. For example, one might only need to marinade the fish for 10 minutes if it were fish fresh off the boat.

Pigeons aux Cerises
Stuffed Pigeons with Morello Sauce

Serves: 8. Total cost: 28 units. Preparation: 45–60 mins. Cooking: 18 mins. Oven: 235°C/455°F/Gas Mk 8. Wine suggestion: Burgundy – Santenay.

Ingredients   8 pigeons
350 g (12 oz) butter
salt and pepper
For the farce:
250 g (9 oz) mushrooms
2 onions
1 clove garlic
50 g (scant 2 oz) butter
20 juniper berries
5 slices white bread soaked in milk and squeezed
salt and pepper
For the sauce:
600 g (about 1¼ lb) black cherries
500 ml (17 fl oz) red wine
200 ml (7 fl oz) consommé
1 soupspoon wine vinegar
2 teaspoons arrowroot
110 g (4 oz) sugar
salt and pepper

Method: Place the cherries in a pan with sugar and enough water to cover. Bring to the boil. Simmer 5 minutes. Drain.

Reduce the red wine, consommé, 150 ml (5 fl oz) cherry syrup and wine vinegar by half. Dissolve the arrowroot in a little cherry syrup. Add to the sauce and continue reduction to a coating consistency. Check seasoning.

Dice the onion and mushroom. Sweat in butter 15 minutes. Combine with crushed juniper berries, crushed garlic, bread and seasoning. Stuff the pigeons.

Rub the pigeons with butter. Season. Roast in a hot oven 18 minutes. Coat with sauce and garnish with cherries.

Rouget au Pistou
Red Mullet with a Herb Paste

Serves: 8. Total cost: 16 units. Preparation: 20–25 mins. Cooking: 6–8 mins. Wine suggestion: Rosé de Provence.

Ingredients   8 red mullet
grilling oil (page 32)
salt and pepper

Method: Wipe the mullet thoroughly. Season inside with salt and pepper. Slightly slit the flesh on both sides of the mullet. Brush with olive oil. Grill for 4 minutes. Turn and grill a further 3 minutes.

Note: The grilling time given relates to a perfectly fresh fish placed over a hot grill. Fish that is not straight out of the nets takes longer.

Pistou

Ingredients   1 soupspoon pine kernels (pignons)
1 soupspoon parmesan cheese
1 soupspoon olive oil
1 large clove garlic
20 leaves fresh basil
sea salt

Method: Pound all the ingredients together in a mortar. The sea salt is abrasive and helps to break down the other ingredients. The pistou is ready once the pine kernels are reduced to a paste.

Either sprinkle small knobs of pistou over the grilled mullet or serve it separately in small pots like a condiment.

Estouffade aux Olives
Ragout of Beef with Black Olives

Serves: 8. Total cost: 25 units. Preparation 25–35 mins. Cooking: 1½ hrs. Wine suggestion: Hermitage rouge.

Ingredients   1350 g (3 lb) chuck steak
250 g (9 oz) belly of pork
3 onions
3 cloves garlic
200 g (7 oz) black olives
1 soupspoon brown sugar
100 ml (3½ fl oz) olive oil
60 g (2 oz) flour
thyme
2 bayleaves
1 litre (1¾ pints) red wine
500 ml (17 fl oz) consommé
salt and pepper

Method: Cube the steak. Trim the belly and cut into domino-sized pieces. Fry the meat a few pieces at a time in oil till well coloured. Sprinkle with the sugar to help the colouring. Reserve. Chop the onion. Fry in the oil.

Return meat to pan. Sprinkle with flour. Allow the flour to colour a little. Moisten with wine and consommé. Add the diced cloves of garlic, a good sprig of thyme and two bayleaves. Simmer covered for 1¼ hours.

Add the olives. Increase the flame. Allow the sauce to reduce for about 15 minutes.

Adjust the seasoning. The dish should need little salt if the olives have been preserved in brine. One will also use less pepper, since the flavour of pepper is stronger when uncooked.

Poulet aux Crevettes

Chicken Stewed in Butter with Prawns

Serves: 8. Total cost: 19 units. Preparation: 20–30 mins. Cooking: stock 15 mins, sauce 20 mins, chicken 1 hr. Oven: 180°C/356°F/Gas Mk 4. Wine suggestion: Chablis.

Ingredients
2 chickens
110 g (4 oz) carrot
110 g (4 oz) onions
110 g (4 oz) celery
80 g (3 oz) butter
40 g (1½ oz) flour
450 ml (16 fl oz) milk
300 ml (10 fl oz) fish stock
400 g (14 oz) cooked prawns
1 level teaspoon turmeric
3 soupspoons cream
salt and pepper

Method: Cut up the chickens into 16 pieces (8 breasts, 8 legs).

Chop the onions, carrot and celery.

Place the butter in a large ovenproof dish with the vegetables on top. Arrange the chicken pieces on the vegetables. Season. Cover the pan and bake in a moderate oven for 1 hour. Remove the pieces of chicken. Wrap in foil and keep warm.

During the cooking of the chicken, shell the cooked prawns. Simmer the shells in the fish stock 15 minutes. Blend in the liquidiser.

When the chicken has been taken out, add the flour to the pan. Pour in the milk to make a velouté-type sauce. Strain the prawn stock into the pan. Simmer 15 minutes. Pass the sauce, without forcing the vegetables, through a sieve or chinois. Add the turmeric. Simmer 5 minutes more. Stir in cream. Bring to the boil and take off the heat.

Return the chicken pieces to the pan together with the shelled prawns. Cover the pan. Allow the chicken to heat through off the flame. Check seasoning.

Epaule d'Agneau à la Berrichonne
Shoulder of Lamb with a Purée of Vegetables

Serves: 8. Total cost: 19 units. Preparation: 30–40 mins. Cooking: 1 hr 50 mins. Wine suggestion: Beaune.

Ingredients   1 shoulder of lamb
200 g (7 oz) minced belly of pork
1 onion
25 g (scant 1 oz) butter
50 g (scant 2 oz) bread soaked in milk and squeezed
1 teaspoon chopped parsley
½ teaspoon allspice
1 egg
1 small clove garlic
salt and pepper
For the purée:
6 leeks
3 sticks celery
500 g (18 oz) celeriac
1 onion
2 carrots
3 potatoes
2 cloves
salt and pepper

Method: Make a stuffing. Mince the belly. Chop the onion and soften in butter. Combine belly, onion, bread, parsley, allspice, diced garlic, egg, salt and pepper.

Spread the farce on the inside of a boned shoulder of lamb. Roll and tie the joint. Place in a large pan. Cover with water. Bring to the boil. Add the leeks, celery, carrot, onion, cloves and salt (about 12 g: scant ½ oz per litre of water). Cover the pan. Simmer 1¼ hours.

Cube the celeriac and the potato. After 1¼ hours add the celeriac. Then 15 minutes later add the potato. Continue simmering till the potatoes are cooked.

Remove all the vegetables from the pan. Blend in the liquidiser. Place them in a fresh pan over a low heat to dry them out a little. (One may lengthen the purée with cream or butter.) Season with pepper.

Untie the joint. Carve pieces as required. Serve on a bed of purée. It may be accompanied with a sauceboat of strained stock.

Poulet Sauté aux Abricots et aux Aubergines

Chicken Sauté with Apricots and Aubergines

Serves: 8. Total cost: 19 units. Preparation: 25–35 mins. Cooking: apricots 30 mins, chicken 12 mins. Wine suggestion: Gamay de Tours.

Ingredients   2 chickens
40 g (1 ½ oz) butter
salt and pepper
For the garnish:
500 g (18 oz) aubergines
350 g (12 oz) apricots (or 200 g (7 oz) dried apricots)
50 ml (1 ¾ fl oz) groundnut oil
1 large onion
1 clove garlic
2 pieces stem ginger
100 ml (3 ½ fl oz) groundnut oil
1 level teaspoon each of ginger, peppercorns, cumin and coriander
4 cardamon pods
salt

Method: Soak the apricots if they are dried. Blanch peel and stone them if they are fresh.

Grind or blend the spices.

Chop the onion. Slice the aubergines. Soften the onion in oil. Add the aubergines. Sauté till they start to colour. Add spices, diced garlic and the ginger finely sliced. Add the apricots. Cover the pan and stew gently for 30 minutes. Season with salt.

Cut up the chickens into 16 pieces. Sauté the breasts in butter 8 minutes and the legs 12 minutes. Arrange them on a bed of apricot and aubergines.

Note: One uses only the cardamon seeds inside the pods. Shell like peas.

Paupiettes de Veau au Genièvre
Veal Paupiettes with a Juniper Sauce

Serves: 8. Total cost: 30 units. Preparation: 45–60 mins. Cooking: paupiettes 20 mins, sauce 30 mins. Oven: 235°C/455°F/Gas Mk 8. Wine suggestion: Bordeaux – Pomerol.

Ingredients   16 × 55 g (2 oz) veal paupiettes (see page 33)
For the juniper berry sauce:
50 g (scant 2 oz) butter
40 g (1 ½ oz) flour
20 juniper berries
200 ml (7 fl oz) white wine
200 ml (7 fl oz) consommé
2 onions
1 soupspoon wine vinegar
150 ml (5 fl oz) cream
salt and pepper

Method: Prepare a coffee coloured roux with the butter and flour. Dice the onion and crush the juniper berries. Add these to the roux. Moisten with the consommé and white wine. Simmer gently 30 minutes. Strain the sauce through a sieve. Add the vinegar. Boil. Add the cream. Check seasoning.

Coat the paupiettes with the sauce.

Limande à la Crème de Carottes
Lemon Sole with a Cream of Carrot Sauce

Serves: 8. Total cost: 20 units. Preparation: 25–35 mins. Cooking: carrots 20 mins, sole 10 mins. Oven: 235°C/455°F/Gas Mk 8. Wine suggestion: Chablis.

Ingredients 450 g (1 lb) carrots
8 lemon soles
1 medium onion
1 large clove garlic
1 soupspoon fresh thyme
1 soupspoon chopped parsley (or chervil)
nutmeg
150 ml (5 fl oz) white wine
100 ml (3½ fl oz) cream
30 g (1 oz) butter
salt and pepper

Method: Slice the carrots. Bring to the boil in a pan of lightly salted water. Simmer till tender.

Sweat finely diced onion in butter.

Set aside 150 g (5½ oz) of the sliced carrots for garnish. Blend the remainder in the liquidiser with onions and a little cooking liquor. The resultant purée should be on the stiff side. Strain through a sieve into a fresh pan. Add crushed garlic and thyme. Re-heat gently.

Fillet the soles. Place rolled fillets in a sauteuse with wine, salt and pepper. Bring to the boil, cover and bake in a hot oven 10 minutes.

Drain the sole. Arrange on a serving dish. Pour a little of their cooking liquor into the sauce. Season with salt, pepper and nutmeg. Finish with cream.

Return sliced carrots to the pan long enough to re-heat.

Coat the fillets with the sauce (it should be a pale, almost pink colour). Garnish with chopped parsley (or chervil) and carrots.

Sweets

N

Tarte à la Menthe

Mint Tart

**Serves: 8. Total cost: 7 units. Preparation: 20–25 mins.
Cooking: 35 mins. Other: resting paste 30 mins. Oven:
180°C/356°F/Gas Mk 4.**

Ingredients		
250 g (9 oz) flour		1 bunch mint
150 g (5½ oz) unsalted butter		4 eggs
1 pinch of salt		100 g (3½ oz) curd cheese
1 large egg		500 ml (17 fl oz)
For the filling:		whipping cream
70 g (scant 3 oz) castor sugar		250 g (9 oz) raisins

Method: Sift the flour and salt. Crumb with the butter. Work in the egg. Roll into a ball. Rest for 20 minutes.

Beat the egg yolks with the sugar in a bowl. Add the curd cheese and continue beating. Whisk the cream till it starts to hold its shape. Fold into the curd, egg and sugar mixture.

Chop the mint.

Whisk the whites till they are in stiff peaks. Fold the raisins, beaten whites and mint into the first mixture.

Line a buttered flan dish with the pastry. Pour the filling on to the pastry case. Bake in a moderate oven 35 minutes till the filling has set.

Picanchagne

Pears Baked en Brioche

**Serves: 8. Total cost: 5 units. Preparation: 25–35 mins. Cooking:
45 mins. Other: proving 1 hr. Oven: 190°C/374°F/Gas Mk 5.**

Ingredients		
60 ml (2 fl oz) milk		35 g (1¼ oz) butter
10 g (⅓ oz) yeast		1 kg (2¼ lb) pears
a pinch of salt		½ lemon
1 egg and 2 yolks		1 teaspoon cinnamon
200 g (7 oz) granulated sugar		1 soupspoon cherry jam
150 g (scant 5 oz) flour		

Method: Heat the milk to body temperature. Place it in a mixing bowl with the yeast. Stir till the yeast dissolves. Add 1 egg and 1 yolk lightly beaten with the pinch of salt to the bowl. Next add 100 g (3½ oz) of sugar, then rain in the flour, beating it with a wooden spoon or dough hook. Melt 30 g (1 oz) butter. Work it into the dough. Place the dough in a warm place to prove for 30 minutes.

Peel half the pears, slice them and moisten them with lemon juice. Peel and cut the rest of the pears into quarters. Poach them for 15 minutes in a pan with 100 g (3½ oz) sugar, cinnamon and cherry jam.

Butter a flan case or tart ring. Spread the dough in the ring. Allow to prove for a further 30 minutes. Arrange the slices of pears in the centre of the dough. Pull up the edge of the dough. Brush with the remaining yolk and place in a moderate oven for 45 minutes.

Drain the poached pears. Reduce the cooking liquor to a syrup.

When the brioche has finished baking, arrange the quarters of poached pears on top. Serve the syrup separately.

Note: This dish has to be eaten the same day as it is baked.

Crêpes aux Framboises
Raspberry Pancakes

Serves: 8. Total cost: 10 units. Preparation: 15–20 mins. Cooking: the pancakes.

Ingredients   pancake batter
(see 'Crêpes fourrées au chocolat' page 144)
450 g (1 lb) raspberries
½ pot of Wilkinson Seeded Raspberry Conserve
1 teaspoon Framboise eau-de-vie
sugar (depending on the sweetness of the raspberries)

Method: Dissolve the sugar in a little water. Heat gently with the raspberry conserve. Place this mixture in a liquidiser with the raspberries. Purée. Sieve. Stir in the alcohol.

Prepare pancakes to order. Spoon a generous amount of the purée over each one. Roll or fold.

195

Sorbet aux Abricots
Apricot Sorbet

Serves: 8. Total cost: 5 units. Preparation: 15–20 mins. Other: browning almonds about 7 mins, to freeze the sorbet 6–8 hrs.

Ingredients   1 kg (2¼ lb) apricots, or 350 g (12 oz) dried apricots
2 lemons
300 g (about 11 oz) granulated sugar
For the garnish:
100 g (3½ oz) flaked almonds
castor sugar
butter

Method: Blanch the apricots 5 minutes in boiling water. Peel and stone them.

Moisten the sugar with a little water. Boil for 2 minutes and cool.

When the syrup has cooled, liquidise the apricots with lemon juice. Add to the syrup. Place in the ice-cream machine and freeze.

Alternatively, place in the freezer till on the point of setting. Remove from freezer. Beat for 2 minutes to break down the crystals and return to the freezer.

Place the almonds on a baking tray. Brush with butter. Bake in a hot oven till they start to colour. Dust with castor sugar. Use to garnish the sorbet.

Note: If using dried apricots, soak them for 1 hour. Blend them in the liquidiser with a little of the water in which they soaked besides the lemon juice.

Biscuit aux Pêches et au Chocolat
Chocolate and Peach Charlotte

Serves: 8. Total cost: 8 units. Preparation: 1–1¼ hrs. Cooking: biscuits 15 mins. Other: to set mould 12 hrs. Oven: 200°C/392°F/Gas Mk 6.

Ingredients   *For the biscuits:*
160 g (5½ oz) castor sugar
4 eggs
115 g (4 oz) flour
vanilla essence
icing sugar
a little rum
For the filling:
180 g (6 oz) plain chocolate
30 g (1 oz) butter
4 eggs
80 g (3 oz) castor sugar
5 peaches poached in syrup
arrowroot

Method: Prepare the biscuits à la cuillère. Beat the sugar and yolks to the ribbon. Add the vanilla essence. Stir in the flour. Beat the whites till stiff. Fold into the mixture. Fill a piping bag (medium size plain tube) with the mixture. Butter sheets of grease-proof paper on baking trays. Pipe 'fingers' of paste 4 cm (1½ inches) apart on the trays. Dredge with icing sugar. Place in a moderate oven for 15 minutes.

Melt the chocolate and butter. Stir in the yolks and castor sugar. Cool. Fold in stiffly beaten whites.

Halve the peaches. Thicken the syrup in which they have cooked with a teaspoon of arrowroot.

Mix a teaspoon of rum with 100 ml (3½ fl oz) water.

Line a charlotte mould with the biscuits à la cuillère. Dip each one in the rum before arranging in place.

Spoon half the chocolate mixture into the mould. Cover with a layer of biscuits. Next a layer of peaches, about 6 halves. Spoon a little thickened syrup over them. Cover with more biscuits. On top add the rest of the chocolate filling. Finish with a layer of biscuits. Place a dish over the mould to weight the filling. Leave in a fridge overnight. Turn out. Blend the rest of the peaches to obtain a purée. Serve as garnish for the 'biscuit'.

Menu 7

October–November

First Courses

Main Courses

Sweets

First Courses

L'Assiette de Charcuterie served with Oignons Confits

Four Meat Pâtés with Glazed Onions

All the quantities for these four recipes are generously estimated, as the pâtés are usually left for the customers to serve themselves. If you serve the portions yourself, they will go further.

Oignons Confits

Glazed Onions

Serves: 8. Total cost: 4 units. Preparation: 15–20 mins. Cooking: 23 mins plus reduction time.

Ingredients   1 kg (2¼ lb) pickling onions
170 g (6 oz) tomato purée
150 ml (5 fl oz) wine vinegar
1 soupspoon olive oil
80 g (3 oz) sugar
100 g (3½ oz) raisins
1 teaspoon curry powder
½ teaspoon coriander
4 cardamon pods
2 bayleaves
salt and pepper

Method: Peel the onions. Blanch 3 minutes in boiling water. Drain.

Mix together wine vinegar, tomato purée and 750 ml (1⅓ pints) water. Bring to the boil. Add the olive oil, sugar, raisins, curry powder, coriander, hulled cardamon seeds, bayleaves, salt and pepper. Simmer 5 minutes.

Poach the whole onions in the liquid for 18 minutes. Drain. Wipe. Reduce the liquid to a glaze. Return the onions to the pan. Shake the pan till they are coated in glaze.

Serve chilled to accompany the following 4 pâtés.

Fromage de Tête
French Brawn

Serves: 12. Total cost: 5 units. Preparation: 30–40 mins. Cooking: 5½ hrs. Other: soaking pig's head 1 hr, cooling stock 1 hr, setting jelly 15 mins, setting meat 30 mins. Wine suggestion: Corbières.

Ingredients   ½ pig's head
3 onions
3 carrots
1 leek
1 stick celery
2 cloves
1 teaspoon allspice
1 clove garlic
2 bayleaves
150 ml (5 fl oz) white wine
1 soupspoon wine vinegar
2 egg whites
salt and pepper

Method: Soak the pig's head in cold water for one hour. Rinse under running water. Place in a large pan. Add the onions, carrots, leek, celery, spices, garlic, bayleaves, wine, vinegar, pepper, a little salt and enough water to cover.

Bring to the boil. Simmer 5 hours. Drain the pig's head. Pull all the meat, fat etc. from the bones. Cube. Avoid handling too much or the meat will turn into a sludge.

Strain the stock. Reduce to about 500 ml (17 fl oz). Whisk a little cooled stock with the whites. Stir into the stock. Return to the boil. Simmer for 30 minutes. Strain the clarified stock through a fine meshed sieve or muslin. Cool.

Pour a third of the stock (which sets to a jelly) in a terrine. Leave to set in freezer for 15 minutes. Mix the rest of the jelly with the meat. Check the seasoning, salt especially. Pour the meat into the terrine. Press down. Leave to set in freezer for 30 minutes. Turn out.

Note: When taking the meat from the bone, remove the tough outer coating of skin from the tongue.

Faude
Belly of Pork Stuffed with Pâté

**Serves: 12. Total cost: 10 units. Preparation: 30–40 mins.
Cooking: 2–2½ hrs. Other: macerating 3 hrs. Oven:
140°C/310°F/Gas Mk 2. Wine suggestion: Beaujolais – St Amour.**

Ingredients   1kg (2¼ lb) belly of pork in a piece
For the farce:
125 g (4½ oz) pig's liver
125 g (4½ oz) minced belly of pork
125 g (4½ oz) minced streaky bacon
125 g (4½ oz) ham
1 large onion
2 cloves garlic
1 level teaspoon allspice
30 g (1 oz) chopped parsley
salt and pepper
1 egg
For braising:
50 g (scant 2 oz) pork dripping
2 onions
2 large carrots
100 ml (3½ fl oz) white wine
500 ml (17 fl oz) chicken stock

Method: Skin and trim the belly. Slide a carving knife through the middle of the piece so that it forms a sleeve (see Falette page 83). Coarsely mince the remaining meats and onion. Combine. Mix in chopped garlic, allspice, parsley and seasoning. Lightly beat the egg and work into the farce. Leave for 3 hours.

Stuff the sleeve of pork belly. Sew up the ends so that the farce is completely enveloped.

Finely dice the onion and carrot. Heat the dripping in a large cocotte. Colour the onion and carrot. Add the pork. Colour the pork. This is important. Not only does the colour improve the finish, it also keeps the meat moist. Deglaze the pan with white wine. Add seasoned stock. Cover. Braise in a low oven for 2½ hours. Cool in the braising stock.

Rillettes d'Oie
Potted Goose

Serves: 24. Total cost: 7 units. Preparation: 15–25 mins. Cooking: 2 hrs. Wine suggestion: Beaujolais – St Amour.

Ingredients   1 goose
salt and pepper

Method: Bone out the goose. Set aside the breast and carcass for a 'Ragoût d'Oie' (page 212). Roughly chop all the leg and wing meat.

Place the fat from round the kidneys in a pan. Melt over a gentle heat. Roughly cut up the goose skin. Add to the pan and allow to stew till the skin has rendered all its fat.

Spoon 150 ml (5 fl oz) of this fat into a large sauteuse. Heat. Add the goose meat and allow to fry until the meat is well coloured. Turn down the heat. Add more of the goose fat, about 350 g (12 oz) per 500 g (18 oz) meat. Leave the meat to stew in this fat for 2 hours till it is almost falling apart.

Drain the meat. Place in a large bowl and flake the meat with a fork or put it through the mincer. Add the fat to the meat. Season. Leave to set.

Use any surplus fat for the ragoût or other meat dishes.

Terrine de Ramiers
Terrine of Wood Pigeon

Serves: 10. Total cost: 11 units. Preparation: 20–25 mins. Cooking: 1¼ hrs. Other: resting 24 hrs. Oven: 190°C/375°F/Gas Mk 5. Wine suggestion: Beaujolais – St Amour.

Ingredients	wood pigeons, enough to	
	give 450 g (1 lb) meat	12 juniper berries
	220 g (8 oz) smoked bacon	1 bayleaf
	220 g (8 oz) bacon ends	1 egg
	100 g (3½ oz) onions	1 soupspoon port
	100 g (3½ oz) mushrooms	salt and pepper
	40 g (1½ oz) butter	(flour and water paste)

Method: Dice the mushrooms and onion. Sweat in the butter. Chop the different meats into small cubes, no bigger than a little fingernail. Add the onion and mushroom duxelles. Crush the juniper berries. Add to the meats. Chop the bayleaf. Add to the meats. Lightly beat the egg with port and seasoning. Add to the meats.

Place the mixture in a terrine. Seal the lid with a flour and water paste. Bake in a moderate oven 1¼ hours. Cool for 2 hours. Remove the lid. Weight the pâté. Leave at least 24 hours before serving.

Note: As an alternative one may bake the mixture in a pastry (see Pâté en croûte page 37). In this case make a standard shortcrust paste based on 500 g (18 oz) flour.

Garbure
Winter Soup

Serves: 8. Total cost: 6 units. Preparation: 15–20 mins. Cooking: 3 hrs. Other: soaking beans 3 hrs. Wine suggestion: any red V.D.Q.S. wine.

Ingredients 350 g (12 oz) belly of port
350 g (12 oz) lean smoked bacon
170 g (6 oz) flageolet beans (or butter beans)
170 g (6 oz) haricot beans
1 savoy cabbage
4 cloves garlic
250 g (9 oz) potatoes
1 soupspoon thyme
1 soupspoon parsley
salt and pepper

Method: Soak both varieties of beans overnight. Dice the belly of pork and the smoked bacon.
Bring 2 litres (3½ pints) water to the boil. Add quartered potatoes, beans, bacon, pork, chopped garlic, thyme, salt and pepper. Simmer 1 hour. Slice the cabbage. Add to the soup. Simmer 2 more hours.

Chop the parsley. Stir into the soup. Serve.

Note: Traditionally, when one makes a garbure, one adds a piece of preserved goose to a soup cooked without the pork and smoked bacon. If one has a little spare rillettes (see Rillettes d'Oie page 205) or goose fat one may add some to the soup. Whisk it into the soup just before serving or the fat will remain on the surface.

Cassolettes de Faisan
Pheasant and Pheasant Dumplings in Sauce

Serves: 8. Total cost: 17 units. Preparation: 30–40 mins. Cooking: pheasant 6 mins, sauce 20 mins, quenelles 10 mins. Other: chilling the forcemeat 1 hr, stock 2 hrs. Wine suggestion: Burgundy – Côte de Beaune.

Ingredients   *For the salpicon:*
breastmeat of 1 pheasant
110 g (4 oz) lean bacon
4 shallots
160 g (6 oz) mushrooms
100 ml (3½ fl oz) port
400 ml (15 fl oz) veal or game stock
2 teaspoon arrowroot
1 teaspoon tomato purée
1 bayleaf
50 ml (1¾ fl oz) groundnut oil
salt and pepper
For the pheasant quenelles:
legs of 1 pheasant
2 slices brown bread
2 egg whites
150 ml (about 4 fl oz) double cream
5 juniper berries
½ teaspoon allspice
salt and pepper
game stock

Method: Prepare some game stock with the carcass and giblets of a pheasant, adding onion, carrot and bouquet garni. About 700 ml (roughly 1¼ pints).

To make the quenelles, purée the boned leg meat. Add the spices and seasoning. Soak the bread in water. Squeeze out as much moisture as possible. Blend with the pheasant. Add the egg whites. Blend again. Place in the fridge 1 hour. Blend chilled cream into the purée.

As required, poach small quenelles (shaped with two teaspoons) in the game stock.

Dice the bacon and pheasant into small cubes. Fry in hot oil. Take out of the pan and set aside. Deglaze the pan with half the port. Add diced shallots and sliced mushrooms. Reduce the stock by two-thirds. Thicken with arrowroot dissolved in a little water. Add to the pan with

207

the tomato purée. Add bayleaf and seasoning. Cook till the sauce is thick and shiny. Stir in the remainder of the port. Off the heat add the pheasant and bacon.

Spoon a little of the salpicon into a cassolette. Place one or two quenelles on top. Coat the quenelles with sauce. Serve.

Moules à la Crème

Mussels with a Cream Sauce

Serves: 8. Total cost: 11 units. Preparation: 15 mins. Cooking: sauce 10 mins. Other: cleaning mussels 20 mins. Wine suggestion: Jurançon.

Ingredients   5 litres (about 1 gallon) mussels
2 shallots
2 branches celery
20 g (¾ oz) butter
400 ml (½ bottle) dry white wine
400 ml (14 fl oz) double cream
1 bayleaf
1 soupspoon chopped parsley
pepper

Method: Dice the shallots and celery. Place them in a large, buttered sauté pan. Add the scrubbed and bearded mussels. Pour over the wine. Heat over a rapid flame (covered). Shake the pan. The mussels have cooked once they have opened. Remove the mussels. Keep warm.

Strain the liquor through muslin (J-cloths make a good substitute). Add bayleaf. Reduce rapidly by two-thirds. Add the cream and continue reducing till the sauce is a coating consistency.

Discard half the mussel shells. Arrange on individual dishes. Stir the parsley into the sauce. Season with pepper only. Spoon the sauce over the mussels.

Pois Chiches à la Navarraise

Baked Chickpeas

Serves: 8. Total cost: 5 units. Preparation: 20–25 mins. Cooking: 2¼ hrs. Other: soaking the chickpeas 12 hrs. Oven: 200°C/392°F/Gas Mk 6. Wine suggestion: Rosé de Provence.

Ingredients   500 g (18 oz) chickpeas
3 onions
100 ml (3 ½ fl oz) olive oil
2 slices stale white bread
450 g (1 lb) tinned tomatoes
2 hard-boiled eggs
2 cloves garlic
1 teaspoon thyme
1 teaspoon rosemary
salt and pepper

Method: Soak the chickpeas overnight.

Place the chickpeas in a large pan of cold salted water. Bring to the boil.
Simmer 2 hours.

Fry the bread in half the olive oil.

Sauté the chopped onions in the remainder of the oil. Add the tomatoes,
thyme and rosemary. Simmer till most of the liquid has evaporated.

Pound the yolks in a mortar with the cloves of garlic. Stir into the
tomato and onion mixture. Check seasoning.

Drain the chickpeas. Add to the sauce. Lengthen with a little of their
cooking liquor. Bake in the oven 15 minutes.

Garnish with diced egg white.

Main Courses

Grillade de Mouton Mariné au Vin Rouge
Marinated Hogget in Red Wine

Serves: 8. Total cost: 27 units. Preparation: 20–30 mins. Cooking: sauce 40 mins, meat 6 mins. Other: marinading 12 hrs. Wine suggestion: Crozes-Hermitage.

Ingredients   1 leg of hogget
300 ml (10 fl oz) red wine
100 ml (3 ½ fl oz) groundnut oil
1 soupspoon allspice
1 large onion
1 carrot
3 bayleaves
80 g (3 oz) butter
salt and pepper
(grilling oil, page 32)

Method: Slice the boned leg into thin collops about 40 g (1 ½ oz) each. Prepare a marinade with sliced onion and carrot, oil, wine, bayleaves and allspice. Lay the slices in the marinade. Leave overnight.

Drain the meat. Wipe with absorbent paper.

Simmer the marinade for 40 minutes, covered. Blend in the liquidiser. Pass through a sieve into a fresh pan. Divide the softened butter into small pieces. Season the marinade. Whisk in the butter. Heat but do not boil.

Brush the slices of lamb with grilling oil. Grill rapidly. The meat in the middle should still be slightly pink. Season.

Pour the sauce made with the marinade over the lamb.

Note: If one puts a piece of meat 1¼ cm (½ in) thick in a marinade for 12 hours, then cuts through it, one will find that the marinade will have barely impregnated the surface of the meat. By cutting fine slices of the meat to be grilled, one ensures that the perfume from the marinade goes almost through the meat.

Ragoût d'Oie

Goose Casserole

**Serves: 10. Total cost: 30 units. Preparation: 25–35 mins.
Cooking: 1¼ hrs plus 45 mins. Wine suggestion: Burgundy –
Chambolle-Musigny.**

Ingredients breast of 1 × 7 kg (16 lb) goose
450 g (1 lb) belly of pork
goose fat
80 g (3 oz) flour
500 ml (18 fl oz) reduced goose stock made from the
    carcass
700 ml (1 bottle) red wine
1 onion
1 clove garlic
450 g (1 lb) button mushrooms
1 large bouquet garni
salt and pepper

Method: Slice the breast of goose into mouthful-sized pieces. Slice the
belly of pork into similar sized pieces.

Heat the fat. Fry the goose and the belly of pork until well-coloured.
Chop the onion and garlic, and add to the pan. Sprinkle the meat with
flour. Shake the pan and allow the flour to colour. Pour over the stock
and then the wine. Add the bouquet garni and salt. Simmer for 1¼ hrs.

Skim off any excess fat that may have separated from the sauce with
kitchen paper. Add the mushrooms. If the sauce has reduced too much,
add extra stock. Continue simmering for a final 45 minutes. Check the
seasoning.

Carré de Porc Provençale

Best End of Pork with Onions and Tomatoes

**Serves: 2. Total cost: 20 units. Preparation: 15–25 mins. Cooking:
coulis 20 mins, pork 20 mins. Other: seasoning meat up to 48 hrs.
Oven: 235°C/455°F/Gas Mk 8. Wine suggestion: Bandol.**

Ingredients 1 × 400 g (14 oz) joint of *For the coulis:*
skinned and trimmed 2 tomatoes
best end of pork 110 g (4 oz) onion
1 teaspoon thyme 1 teaspoon Herbes de
½ teaspoon sage Provence
1 bayleaf 1 soupspoon olive oil
1 clove garlic salt and pepper
50 ml (1¾ fl oz) olive oil
sea salt and pepper

Method: Score the fat on the joint of pork without damaging the flesh. Mix together herbs, garlic crushed with sea salt, pepper and olive oil. Rub this mixture over the pork. Leave as long as possible (even up to 48 hours).

Place the joint on a cooling rack. Roast in a very hot oven 20 minutes. Dice the onion. Sweat in olive oil till transparent. Add roughly diced, skinned tomatoes, Herbes de Provence and seasoning. Allow to cook gently for 20 minutes.

Serve the coulis with the pork. One may mix the juices rendered by the pork into the coulis.

Boeuf Sauté aux Anchois
Beef Sauté with Anchovies

Serves: 8. Total cost: 22 units. Preparation: 20–25 mins. Cooking: 1¾ hrs. Wine suggestion: Bordeaux – St Emilion.

Ingredients 1350 g (3 lb) chuck steak
8 cloves garlic
100 ml (3½ fl oz) olive oil
60 g (2 oz) flour
50 g (scant 2 oz) sugar
1 small tin of anchovies
500 ml (17 fl oz) consommé
500 ml (17 fl oz) red wine
100 ml (3½ fl oz) sherry
salt and pepper

Method: Cube the meat. Sauté in olive oil till well coloured. Add the sugar to the pan while the meat is colouring for a darker finish. Stir in the flour. Allow to cook 5 minutes. Add the wine and consommé. Add

diced garlic. Bring to the boil. Cover. Simmer 1 hour. Pound the
anchovies. Beat into the sauce. Continue simmering 45 minutes more.
Check the seasoning. Add sherry.

Lapin Farci aux Champignons
Boned Rabbit Stuffed with Mushrooms

**Serves: 8. Total cost: 12 units. Preparation: 45–60 mins. Cooking:
1¼ hrs. Oven: 200°C/392°F/Gas Mk 6. Wine suggestion: Bordeaux
– St Emilion.**

Ingredients   1350 g (3 lb) rabbit pulled and skinned
200 g (7 oz) mushrooms
200 g (7 oz) minced veal
100 g (3½ oz) minced back bacon
1 egg
1 teaspoon powdered sage
bacon fat
salt and pepper

Method: Bone the rabbit. This is a long job and a fiddly one because
of the small rabbit bones. Using the tip of a knife ease the meat away
from the two leg bones. Repeat with the meat on the forelegs. Cut
through the middle of the carcass from the gutted stomach to the neck.
Free the flank and fillets from the rib cage and backbone. Now detach
the aitch bone. At this point one can lift the bones away and the flesh
will be in one piece, hopefully not too damaged.

Slice the mushrooms. Combine the minced veal, bacon, mushrooms,
sage, diced rabbit liver, egg, salt and pepper. Spread this farce on the
inside of the rabbit.

Take a needle and thread. Re-shape the rabbit as far as possible,
arranging the hind legs on either side of the body. Sew up the rabbit to
contain the farce. Brush with bacon fat. Wrap in foil. Bake in a hottish
oven 1¼ hours.

Remove from the oven. Pull out the thread. Cool slightly. Carve
vertical slices as one would with a galantine.

Note: For the sauce: add 200 g (7 oz) of field mushrooms to 400 ml
(14 fl oz) Madeira sauce (page 41). Simmer 7 minutes. Whisk in any
juices rendered by the rabbit during cooking.

Goulasch

Hungarian Stew

Serves: 8. Total cost: 23 units. Preparation: 20–30 mins. Cooking: 1 hr 35 mins. Wine suggestion: Hungarian Cabernet.

Ingredients   1350 g (about 3 lb) chuck steak
5 onions
2 carrots
1 branch celery
60 g (2 oz) paprika
2 tomatoes
1 soupspoon brown sugar
60 g (2 oz) flour
100 ml (3½ fl oz) groundnut oil
bouquet garni
600 ml (1 pint) consommé
600 ml (1 pint) red wine
salt and pepper

Method: Chop the meat into large cubes. Fry them a few pieces at a time in oil till well coloured. Sprinkle with brown sugar to help the colouring. Dice the onion, carrot and celery. Fry them in the oil till coloured.

Return the meat to the pan. Stir in the flour and allow to brown. Add the paprika. Shake the pan well. Allow it to cook for 3 minutes. Moisten with the consommé and wine. Add the bouquet garni. Bring to the boil. Simmer for 1¼ hrs.

Blanch and peel the tomatoes. Dice them and add to the goulasch. Simmer for a further 20 minutes. Check the seasoning.

Serve the goulasch with a bowl of sour cream.

Note: 'Goulasch' as far as the author knows is simply a central European word for stew. It just happens to be an excellent combination – paprika and beef. Recipes for goulasch, and plenty exist, tend to use white wine and more tomatoes than are given in this recipe. They also use less paprika.

Though the quantity of paprika one uses is determined by its quality, it should be the star flavour in the sauce. Look at its colour before use and the reader will realise why a red wine is more suitable. White wine and more tomatoes give a bright 'cayenne' colour to the sauce. Red wine gives a deep red or auburn tint.

Bourride
Baked Fish with a Garlic and Butter Sauce

Serves: 8. Total cost: 19 units. Preparation: 25–35 mins. Cooking: 15 mins. Oven: 235°C/455°F/Gas Mk 8. Wine suggestion: Burgundy – Rully.

Ingredients
8 small whiting fillets
8 small hake steaks
8 skinned bream fillets
500 ml (17 fl oz) fish stock
220 g (8 oz) tinned tomatoes
zest of half an orange
4 cloves garlic
400 ml (14 fl oz) Hollandaise sauce (page 40)
salt and pepper
(croûtons made with slices of French bread
fried in olive oil)

Method: Arrange the fish on a shallow tray. Liquidise the tomatoes, the fish stock and the garlic. Pour this mixture over the fish. Season. Add zest. Bring to the boil. Cover with foil. Bake in a hot oven 15 minutes. Drain the fish. Keep warm.

Have some Hollandaise ready in a bowl over a bain–marie. Whisk in a third of the cooking liquor from the fish.

Serve the fish on croûtons. Coat with a little of the sauce. Serve the rest of the sauce separately.

Note: This recipe is an adaptation of a Provençal fish stew. Nearly all recipes that the author has seen for this dish use aioli (a mayonnaise prepared with hard-boiled yolks and crushed garlic). Living in the North we do not have the same fish as in the Mediterranean. Hollandaise, a butter compound sauce, is probably a better accompaniment for the more delicate white fish that we tend to have available in our shops. One is free to select whatever fish one likes for a bourride.

Langue de Veau aux Cornichons
Veal Tongue with Gherkin Sauce

Serves: 8. Total cost: 13 units. Preparation: 15–20 mins. Cooking: 2½ hrs. Other: soaking 3 hrs. Wine suggestion: Bordeaux – red Graves.

Ingredients   1 veal tongue
1 litre (35 fl oz) consommé
100 ml (3 ½ fl oz) red wine
3 bayleaves
3 cloves
2 soupspoons wine vinegar
2 teaspoons arrowroot
110 g (4 oz) pickled gherkins
1 shallot
1 soupspoon chopped parsley
salt and pepper

Method: Soak the tongue 3 hours in cold water.

Place the tongue in a pan with consommé, wine, bayleaves, cloves and enough water to cover. Bring to the boil. Simmer 2½ hours.

Strain 500 ml (17 fl oz) of the cooking liquor into a fresh pan. Dissolve the arrowroot in the wine vinegar. Add to the liquor. Reduce by a third. Dice the shallot. Slice the gherkins into fine rings. Add to the sauce. Simmer 5 minutes more. Stir in chopped parsley. Check seasoning.

Drain the tongue. Remove the leathery coating on the tongue. Carve into slices. Coat with a little sauce. Serve the remainder of the sauce separately in a sauce boat.

Sweets

Tarte aux Raisins
Grape Tart

Serves: 8. Total cost: 7 units. Preparation: 30–35 mins. Cooking: 30 mins. Other: cooling crème 1 hr. Oven: 180°C/356°F/Gas Mk 4.

Ingredients 250 g (9 oz) white grapes
250 g (9 oz) black grapes
80 g (3 oz) sugar
For the crème:
80 g (3 oz) sugar
4 yolks
40 g (1½ oz) flour
300 ml (10 fl oz) milk
a few drops of vanilla
For the pâté brisée:
250 g (9 oz) flour
125 g (4½ oz) butter

Method: Make the paste. Crumb the flour and butter. Add enough water to make a smooth paste. Roll into a ball. Rest. Butter a tart ring. Roll out the paste. Line the tart ring. Bake blind in a moderate oven for 25 minutes. Remove the paper and baking beans. Bake a further 5 minutes.

Make a crème. Beat sugar, yolks, vanilla essence and flour. Pour over the hot milk. Stir. Place the crème in a pan. Bring to the boil stirring continuously. Cool. Spread over the pastry.

Make a syrup with the sugar and 200 ml (7 fl oz) water. Poach both sorts of grapes in the syrup for 5 minutes. Drain. Wipe. Arrange alternate rings of black and white grapes in the tart.

Reduce the syrup to a glaze. Coat the grapes with the glaze.

Poires à la Crème
Pears Baked with Cream

Serves: 8. Total cost: 8 units. Preparation: 15 mins. Cooking: 1 hr. Oven: 175°C/347°F/Gas Mk 4.

Ingredients   8 firm pears, (Williams, Bartlett's etc. – not Conference)
80 g (3 oz) soft brown sugar
600 ml (1 pint) double cream
cinnamon
1 soupspoon pear eau-de-vie

Method: Peel, core and slice the pears. Place them in layers in an ovenproof dish, preferably on the shallow side. Sprinkle each layer with cinnamon, sugar and a dash of eau-de-vie. Pour over the cream. Bake in a moderate oven for 1 hour. The dish is ready once the cream has thickened.

Note: If the pears are on the juicy side, wipe them before arranging them in the ovenproof dish.

Tarte de Mme Cavaf
Apricot and Walnut Meringue Tart

Serves: 8. Total cost: 7 units. Preparation: 25–35 mins. Cooking: 25 mins plus 40 mins. Other: soaking apricots 2 hrs, resting paste 30 mins. Oven: 25 mins at 180°C/356°F/Gas Mk 4, 40 mins at 120°C/248°F/Gas Mk ¼.

Ingredients   *For the pastry:*
250 g (9 oz) flour
200 g (7 oz) butter
100 g (3½ oz) castor sugar
2 eggs
For the filling:
220 g (8 oz) walnuts
220 g (8 oz) dried Turkish apricots
350 g (12 oz) castor sugar
4 eggs

Method: Prepare a sweet paste with the flour, sugar, butter and eggs. Roll into a ball and rest.

Soak the apricots in water for 2 hours. Stew them in water with 110 g (4 oz) sugar. Drain. Blend to a purée.

Roughly chop the walnuts. Add half to the apricot purée.

Separate the whites and the yolks.

Prepare a meringue with the whites and the rest of the sugar. Combine the yolks and the rest of the walnuts. Fold them into the meringue.

Line a buttered flan ring with the pastry. Spread the apricot purée on top. Spoon the meringue mixture to cover the apricots.

Place in a moderate oven for 25 minutes. Turn the oven temperature down as low as possible and leave the tart till the meringue has dried out – approximately 40 minutes more.

Serve cold.

Note: It is sometimes possible to buy ducks' eggs. They are especially useful in preparing items of pâtissèrie, pastry, meringue, crèmes etc.

Pouding de Marrons
Chestnut Pudding

Serves: 8. Total cost: 10 units. Preparation: 25–35 mins. Cooking: 40 mins. Other: poaching the chestnuts about 45 mins. Oven: 175°C/374°F/Gas Mk 5.

Ingredients   1 kg (2¼ lb) chestnuts
700 ml (25 fl oz) milk
1 vanilla pod
150 g (5½ oz) sugar
100 g (3½ oz) ground almonds
8 marrons glacés
icing sugar
60 g (2 oz) butter
6 eggs

Method: Split the skins of the chestnuts. Blanch 10 minutes in boiling water. Drain. Peel.

Poach the chestnuts in milk with the vanilla pod. They are cooked once they have absorbed all the liquid. Purée. Add the sugar, the ground almonds, softened butter and egg yolks.

Stiffly beat the whites. Fold them into the mixture.

Pour into a buttered charlotte mould. Place the mould in a bain-marie. Bake in a warm oven 40 minutes.

Cool. Turn out the pudding. Sprinkle with icing sugar. Garnish with marrons glacés.

Ginger Ice-cream

Serves: 8. Total cost: 9 units. Preparation: 15–20 mins. Other: freezing 6 hrs.

Ingredients   150 g (5 oz) stem ginger in syrup
1 heaped teaspoon powdered ginger
900 ml (1 ½ pints) double cream
8 yolks
220 g (8 oz) castor sugar

Method: Purée the stem ginger, its syrup, the powdered ginger and 100 ml (3 ½ fl oz) cream.

Beat the yolks and castor sugar till stiff. They are ready if they fold like a ribbon when poured off the spatula.

Beat the rest of the cream till it holds its shape on the whisk. Add the yolks and sugar mix. Stir in the ginger purée.

Place in the freezer till on the point of setting. Remove and beat again. Return to the freezer.

Flan à la Pâte de Noisettes

Hazelnut Flan

Serves: 8. Total cost: 9 units. Preparation: 25–30 mins. Cooking: 25 mins. Other: resting paste 30 mins, chilling flan 1 hr. Oven: 200°C/392°F/Gas Mk 6.

Ingredients   375 g (12 ½ oz) hazelnut paste (from health food stores)
80 g (3 oz) honey
50 g (scant 2 oz) chopped hazelnuts
5 eggs
150 ml (5 fl oz) cream
1 teaspoon ginger
(butter)
For the paste:
250 g (9 oz) flour
150 g (5 ½ oz) butter
80 g (3 oz) castor sugar
1 large egg

Method: Make a pâte sablée. Crumb flour and the butter. Mix eggs and sugar. Blend into flour. Work into a paste. Rest 30 minutes. Butter a flan ring. Line with the paste.

Combine hazelnut paste, honey, eggs, chopped hazelnuts, cream and ginger. Spread the mixture on the pâte sablée. Bake in a hottish oven for 25 minutes till the filling has set. Chill.

Menu 8

November–December

First Courses

Main Courses

Sweets

First Courses

Boudin Blanc aux Pommes
White Pudding with Apples

Serves: 8. Total cost: 10 units. Preparation: 35–45 mins. Cooking: 25 mins. Other: chilling 1 hr. Wine suggestion: Riesling.

Ingredients   450 g (1 lb) cooked chicken or turkey breast
1 calf's sweetbread
60 g (2 oz) rice
250 ml (9 fl oz) milk
50 ml (1 ¾ fl oz) cream
1 egg
nutmeg
salt and pepper
2 m (6 ft 6 in) of sausage skins
For poaching the boudins:
1 litre (35 fl oz) milk (or chicken stock)

Method: Soak the sweetbread in running water. Blanch 10 minutes. Remove any gristle or fat. Boil the rice in 250 ml (9 fl oz) milk. When cooked, blend rice and meats as finely as possible. Chill. Blend in egg, cream, nutmeg, salt and pepper. Fill a piping bag (plain tube) with the mixture. Leaving enough skin at each end to tie a knot, fill the sausage skins. Do not overcharge because the boudin swells during cooking.

Poach the boudins in simmering milk for 25 minutes. Cool. When re-heating, wrap each boudin in cooking film (or foil) slightly oiled. Re-heat in the oven.

Note: There is no single, standard recipe for boudin blanc. One can make it with veal, with chicken, or with pork. As an alternative one could prepare a quenelle mixture and use that to fill the skins.

The dish is best served with an apple sauce. Peel 1 kg (2¼ lb) of apples and stew in 60 g (2 oz) butter.

Filets de Turbot au Pouilly
Turbot with a Pouilly-Fuissé Sauce

Serves: 8. Total cost: 13 units. Preparation: 15–25 mins. Cooking: 6 mins plus 7 mins. Oven: 204°C/425°F/Gas Mk 7. Wine suggestion: Pouilly-Fuissé.

Ingredients 2 small turbots
400 ml (14 fl oz) fish stock
2 shallots
40 g (1 ½ oz) unsalted butter
250 ml (8 ½ fl oz) Pouilly-Fuissé
220 g (8 oz) mushrooms
4 tomatoes
1 soupspoon cream
150 ml (5 fl oz) Hollandaise sauce
salt and pepper

Method: Lift and skin the turbot fillets. Roll them like a Swiss Roll. They should weigh about 110 g (4 oz) each.

Bring the stock to the boil and reduce by half.

Butter a large ovenproof dish. Chop shallots. Slice mushrooms. Add to the pan. Arrange the turbot fillets on top. Cover with foil. Bake in a hot oven 6 minutes. Add the stock and white wine. Bring to the boil on top of the oven. Return to the oven to finish cooking (about 7 more minutes). Drain the fillets and mushrooms. Arrange on a fresh buttered serving dish. Cover with foil. Keep warm.

Blanch, skin and liquidise the tomatoes (not tinned here; they contain too much moisture). Add to the cooking liquor. Reduce by half. Strain. Add cream. Whisk into the Hollandaise. Check seasoning. Coat the turbot with the sauce. Glaze under the salamander/grill.

Garnish with fleurons (puff pastry crescents).

Omelette aux Coques
Cockle Omelette

Serves: 8. Total cost: 10 units. Preparation: 20–25 mins. Cooking: 10 mins plus omelettes. Wine suggestion: Pilton or Thornbury Castle.

Ingredients 1 ½ litres (about 2 ¾ pints) cockles
1 soupspoon chopped celery leaves
1 onion
110 g (4 oz) butter
16 eggs
2 yolks
200 ml (7 fl oz) white wine
100 ml (3 ½ fl oz) cream
salt and pepper

Method: Scrub the fresh cockles as one would do with mussels. Dice the onion. Sweat the onions in a large pan in 50 g (scant 2 oz) butter. Add celery leaves, wine and pepper. Place the cockles on top. Bring the liquid to the boil. Cover. Simmer for about 10 minutes till the cockles have opened.

Strain the cooking liquid through muslin. Shell the cockles.

Beat together the 2 yolks and cream. Whisk in 3 soupspoons of cockle liquor. Place the sauce in a bain-marie. Stir in the cockles. Keep warm.

Beat the eggs. Season.

Butter an omelette pan. Prepare eight omelettes. As each omelette cooks, spoon some cockles and sauce on to it. Fold the omelette. Serve.

Note: There are two schools of omelette makers: those who like them golden and those who feel they should not be allowed to colour. It does not matter which one adopts. However, it takes less than a minute to cook an omelette. To do this one needs a hot pan and clarified butter. Unless the butter is clarified, the salt will burn and the omelette spoil. Brush the hot pan with butter. Pour in the omelette mixture. Let it sit in the pan for 10 seconds. Shake the pan vigorously. Tilt it both towards and away from you. Let the cooked omelette slip to the bottom of the pan away from the handle. Spread the filling. Fold the omelette in half. Slide on to a plate. Serve at once.

Pâté de Lièvre Chaud
Hot Hare Pâté

Serves: 10. Total cost: 12 units. Preparation: 1 hr. Cooking: stock 2 hrs, pâté 1½ hrs. Oven: 15 mins at 220°C/428°F/Gas Mk 7, 1¼ hrs at 200°C/392°F/Gas Mk 6. Wine suggestion: Bordeaux – St Julien.

Ingredients 1 young hare prepared weight 2 kg (4½ lb)
40 g (1½ oz) butter
1 teaspoon chopped sage
3 juniper berries
3 slices of white bread soaked in game stock (see below)
    and squeezed to expel excess moisture
salt and pepper
(oil for stiffening fillets)
For the paste:
500 g (17 oz) flour
300 g (11 oz) butter
2 eggs
1 yolk
For the sauce:
1 bottle red Bordeaux
hare bones
2 onions
2 carrots
bouquet garni
1 soupspoon meat or game glaze
1 egg white
2 teaspoons arrowroot
salt and pepper

Method: Make a rich shortcrust pastry with flour, butter and whole eggs. Rest.

Mince the leg meat from the hare. Slice the fillets into 5 cm (2 in) lengths. Chop the liver.

Brown the hare bones in the oven. Add chopped onion, sliced carrot and bouquet garni. Pour over the wine and an equal quantity of water. Bring to the boil. Simmer gently for 2 hours. Strain the stock. Reduce to about two-thirds of its original volume. Whisk the white of an egg lightly with a little cooled stock. Stir into the stock off the heat. Return to the heat. Stir till the stock begins to simmer. Leave 20 minutes for the clarification.

Strain through muslin. Dissolve the arrowroot in a little wine or water. Add to the clarified sauce. Bring to the boil. Check the seasoning.

Butter a charlotte mould. Line with the pastry.

Mix the bread, the minced leg meat, meat glaze, melted butter and chopped liver. Add crushed juniper berries, sage and seasoning.

Stiffen the fillets by frying them briefly in hot oil.

Fill the lined mould with the pâté mixture. Press the fillets vertically into this farce. Cover with a layer of paste. Carefully seal the edges.

Glaze with egg yolk. Make a chimney for steam to escape. Place in a hot oven 15 minutes. Turn down to moderate for a further 1¼ hrs.

Serve warm accompanied by hot sauce.

Pâté de Faisan
Pheasant Pâté

Serves: 10. Total cost: 15 units. Preparation: 20–30 mins. Cooking: 1½ hrs. Other: marinading 12 hrs, resting cooked pâté 24 hrs. Oven: 190°C/375°F/Gas Mk 7. Wine suggestion: Beaujolais – Morgon.

Ingredients   1 pheasant (cock or hen)
150 g (5½ oz) smoked bacon
350 g (12–13 oz) trimmed belly of pork
1 onion
100 g (3½ oz) mushrooms
100 ml (3½ fl oz) port
2 cloves garlic
7 juniper berries
2 bayleaves
30 g (1 oz) butter
salt and pepper
(1 strip of bacon rind)
(flour and water paste)

Method: Bone the pheasant. Prepare a stock with neck, giblets, carcass and bones. Reduce the stock to a glaze (see page 24).

Mince the leg-meat, one breast, bacon, belly of pork, onion and mushrooms.

Slice the remaining breast into slivers. Leave overnight in a marinade of port, crushed garlic, juniper berries, bayleaves, salt and pepper.

Strain the marinade. Mix it into the farce with melted butter and slivers of pheasant.

Place a bayleaf from the marinade on the bottom of a terrine. Cover with the strip of bacon rind. Fill the terrine with the farce. Place the other bayleaf on top.

Prepare a flour and water paste, the texture of putty. Use a ribbon of this paste to seal the lid of the terrine. Place in a bain-marie and bake in a moderate oven for 1 ½ hours.

Take out of the oven and cool for 2 hours. Remove the lid. Weight the pâté. Leave 24 hours. Pour the glaze on the point of setting over the pâté.

Matefaim aux Oignons
Onion Pancake

Serves: 8. Total cost: 11 units. Preparation: 20–25 mins. Cooking: 6 mins. Other: to rest the batter 1 hr. Wine suggestion: Pinot-Chardonnay.

Ingredients   1 kg (2¼ lb) potatoes
1 ½ kg (3 ½ lb) onions
300 ml (10 fl oz) double cream
12 eggs
150 g (5 ½ oz) butter
1 soupspoon flour
100 ml (3 ½ fl oz) groundnut oil
salt and pepper

Method: Boil the potatoes in their skins. Peel, sieve and allow them to cool. Slice the onions and fry them in half the butter and oil. Keep warm. Mix the potato and flour. Add the yolks one by one. Stir in cream. Season. Beat the egg whites to soft peaks. Fold into the mixture.

This batter is to be made into pancakes. For individual servings fry two pancakes in a small sauteuse. For two to four portions use a correspondingly larger pan, with increased quantities of batter.

Put a layer of the fried onion between two pancakes. Serve.

Note: Recipes in this book are generally more digestible than this one which is almost a winter high tea by itself. The first time that the author attempted this dish, he added whole eggs to the flour/potato mix. By separating them and folding in the whites afterwards, he hopes that the dish will not be too overpowering as part of an evening meal.

233

Dèlices au Fromage
Deep-fried Gruyère and Egg White

Serves: 8. Total cost: 4 units. Preparation: 15–20 mins. Cooking: 5 mins. Other: chilling whites 1 hr. Wine suggestion: Moselle.

Ingredients
4 egg whites
200 g (7 oz) grated Gruyère
120 g (about 4 oz) white breadcrumbs
1 level coffeespoon nutmeg
salt and pepper
(deep-frying oil)

Method: Stiffly beat the egg whites.

Season the grated Gruyère heavily because of the blandness in the whites. Fold the beaten whites into the cheese and nutmeg. Chill. Mould the mixture into small balls, using two teaspoons. Roll the balls in breadcrumbs. Deep-fry in hot oil 5 minutes. Drain.

Serve with a Choron sauce (see page 63).

Note: This simple dish offers an excellent way of using up the egg whites that so often stand around a professional kitchen. It is worth mentioning that whites that are not quite fresh beat better than those straight from the hen.

Stilton Soup

Serves: 8. Total cost: 6 units. Preparation: 15–20 mins. Cooking: 30 mins. Wine suggestion: dependent on main course.

Ingredients
220 g (8 oz) Stilton
2 sticks celery
1 medium onion
1 litre (35 fl oz) chicken stock
100 ml (3½ fl oz) white wine
100 ml (3½ fl oz) cream
50 g (scant 2 oz) flour
50 g (scant 2 oz) butter
1 teaspoon chopped thyme
salt and pepper

Method: Make a roux with flour and butter. Pour over the stock. Bring to the boil. Add the thyme, whole onion and celery. Simmer gently 20 minutes. Add the wine.

Grate the Stilton. Stir into soup. Simmer 10 minutes more. Check seasoning. Remove the sticks of celery and onion. Add the cream. Return to the boil. Serve.

Main Courses

Poulet aux Noix et aux Raisins
Chicken with Walnuts and Grapes

Serves: 8. Total cost: 18 units. Preparation: 15–20 mins. Cooking: chicken 12 mins, sauce 6 mins. Wine suggestion: Rupertsberger.

Ingredients   2 chickens
100 ml (3½ fl oz) groundnut oil
30 g (1 oz) butter
170 g (6 oz) liquid acacia honey
250 g (9 oz) walnuts
250 g (9 oz) white grapes
salt and pepper

Method: Cut up the chicken (8 pieces of breast, 8 pieces of leg). Season. Brush with liquid honey. Heat the oil and butter. Sauté the chicken skin side down for 9 minutes, then 3 minutes on the other side. Remove from the pan and keep warm.

Add the rest of the honey to the pan with walnuts. Sauté for 4 minutes. Add the grapes and continue to sauté until the grapes have heated through, about 2 minutes.

Serve the chicken pieces on a bed of walnuts and raisins.

Note: Note the quality of the dish will be improved if one replaces the groundnut with walnut oil.

Mousseline de Poisson à la Crème de Homard
Fish Mousseline with Lobster Sauce

Serves: 8. Total cost: 24 units. Preparation: 40–50 mins. Cooking: lobster 20 mins, sauce 20 mins, mousseline 15 mins. Other: to chill the mousseline 1 hr. Wine suggestion: Montrachet.

Ingredients   500 g (17 oz) whiting fillets
4 egg whites
500 ml (18 fl oz) double cream
1 soupspoon chopped parsley
1 teaspoon nutmeg
1 heaped teaspoon salt
1 level teaspoon ground white pepper
(butter)
For the crème de homard:
1 small lobster
110 g (4 oz) leeks
110 g (4 oz) parsnips
90 g (generous 3 oz) butter
30 g (1 oz) flour
100 ml (3½ fl oz) milk
50 ml (1¾ fl oz) double cream
100 ml (3½ fl oz) Hollandaise sauce (page 40)
salt and pepper

Method: Dice the leeks and parsnips. Sweat them in 50 g (scant 2 oz) butter till the parsnips start to colour. Place the lobster whole on this bed of vegetables. Cover with water (or fish stock). Season heavily. Bring to the boil and poach 20 minutes.

Liquidise all the lobster meat except for one half of the tail with 100 ml (3½ fl oz) cooking liquor. Transfer to a bowl. Put the shell in a fine sieve. Hold it over this bowl. Press as much juice as possible into it. (Reserve any coral for the Congre à l' Américaine, page 241.)

Prepare a blond roux with the rest of the butter and the flour. Add the milk and 300 ml (10 fl oz) of lobster bouillon, a third at a time. Simmer 20 minutes. Add the blended lobster meat and juices.

Stir the cream into a stiffish Hollandaise over a bain-marie. Whisk in the lobster sauce a little at a time. Dice the rest of the tail-meat and add it to the sauce. Keep hot, but do not boil.

Blend the fish in the liquidiser. Add the whites, parsley, nutmeg and the seasoning. Continue blending till quite smooth. Chill. Blend in chilled cream.

Butter sixteen poaching moulds. Spoon the mousseline into each mould. Poach till the mousseline sets, about 15 minutes. Serve two per portion. Coat with the sauce.

Note: One may replace the mousseline mixture with a standard quenelle mixture (see page 35) which is more economical.

Potée Bretonne
Boiled Duck, Mutton and Pork

Serves: 8. Total cost: 22 units. Preparation: 25–35 mins. Cooking: 2½ hrs. Wine suggestion: Gigondas.

Ingredients   600 g (21 oz) boned shoulder of lamb or hogget
350 g (12 oz) boned belly of pork
2 kg (4½ lb) duck
1 large cabbage
5 leeks
3 carrots
6 small turnips or parsnips
1 kg (2¼ lb) potatoes
4 tomatoes
2 soupspoons thyme
50 g (scant 2 oz) butter
salt and pepper

Method: Slice the cabbage. Roughly chop the leeks. Peel and quarter the turnips or parsnips. Slice the carrots. Peel and quarter the potatoes. Blanch and skin the tomatoes.

Heat the butter in a pan. Sauté the duck on all sides till it has coloured.

Place the carrots, leek and cabbage in a large pan. Place the belly, the shoulder of lamb or hogget and the duck on top. Cover with water and bring to the boil. Add thyme. Season. Simmer 2½ hours.

One hour before serving add the turnips or parsnips. Half an hour before serving add the tomatoes and potatoes.

Serve the vegetables from a soup tureen. Serve the meat from a separate dish.

Note: Unless eight portions are ordered for a single party, serving and maintaining the dish in peak condition demands a degree of planning. Every establishment will find its own solution. The author suggests that once the dish has been prepared, remove the meat and keep warm in a pan of stock, placed in a bain-marie. The vegetables can be kept warm and re-heated to order.

Mouton Sauté aux Citrons
Hogget Sauté with Lemons

Serves: 8. Total cost: 24 units. Preparation: 20–25 mins. Cooking: 1½ hrs. Wine suggestion: Sauternes perhaps – this dish is rather hard to match with a wine.

Ingredients   1 small leg of hogget
100 ml (3½ fl oz) groundnut oil
5 lemons (not with thick skins)
1 teaspoon allspice
1 level coffeespoon nutmeg
1 teaspoon turmeric
50 ml (1¾ fl oz) rum
200 ml (7 fl oz) Moselle or Barsac
2 teaspoons arrowroot
salt and pepper

Method: Bone the mutton and cut into 2½ cm (1 in) cubes. Sauté a few pieces at a time in hot oil. Colour well. Add the rum. Flame. Sprinkle with turmeric and allow this spice to cook for 2 minutes. Pour over the lemon juice and white wine. Bring to the boil. Add the allspice, nutmeg, salt and pepper. Simmer 1½ hours. (Lengthen with boiling water if necessary.)

Dissolve the arrowroot in a little of the sauce. Add to the pan. Bring to the boil.

Serve with boiled rice.

Côte de Porc au Vin Rouge
Pork Baked with Red Wine

Serves: 8. Total cost: 19 units. Preparation: 15–20 mins. Cooking: 20 mins. Oven: 190°C/374°F/Gas Mk 5. Wine suggestion: Chinon.

Ingredients

8 large pork chops (from the best end)	24 juniper berries
200 ml (7 fl oz) consommé	200 ml (7 fl oz) cream
200 ml (7 fl oz) red wine	80 g (3 oz) butter
2 bayleaves	60 g (2 oz) flour
	salt and pepper

240

Method: Season the flour. Dust the pork on both sides. Sauté the chops in butter till they have coloured. Place in an ovenproof dish. Deglaze the pan with consommé and wine. Bring to the boil. Pour over the pork. Add bayleaves, juniper berries, salt and pepper. Bake in a moderate oven 20 minutes.

Place the chops on serving dishes. Add cream to the sauce. Reduce rapidly. Strain over the meat.

Congre à l'Américaine
Conger Eel with an Américaine Sauce

Serves: 8. Total cost: 28 units. Preparation: 35–45 mins. Cooking: 25 mins. Wine suggestion: Pouilly-Fumé.

Ingredients   8 × 200 g (7 oz) conger steaks taken from the head
450 g (1 lb) lobster
450 g (1 lb) tinned tomatoes
2 onions
2 carrots
300 ml (10 fl oz) white wine
300 ml (10 fl oz) fish stock
100 g (3½ oz) butter
100 ml (3½ fl oz) olive oil
3 soupspoons cognac
3 soupspoons chopped parsley
salt and pepper

Method: Prepare the lobster. Split the lobster's head with a large chopping knife. Detach the claws and legs from the body. Separate the tail from the body. Discard the stomach sacs. Remove coral and the creamy intestine substance and reserve. Crack the claws with a hammer. Slice the tail into natural sections.

Bone the conger steaks. Tie them into steaks again, using kitchen string.

Heat olive oil in a large sauteuse. Sauté the pieces of lobster. Set aside. Sauté the pieces of conger till they begin to colour.

Dice the onion and carrot finely. Sweat in the oil for 5 minutes. Return lobster to the pan. Pour over the cognac. Flame. Season. Add the white wine and stock.

Seed the tomatoes. Strain any excess moisture. Chop roughly. Add to the pan. Simmer 25 minutes. If the sauce seems too liquid, one may reduce it at this time.

Q

Liquidise the intestine, coral, softened butter and a soupspoon of stock.

Remove the lobster pieces from the pan and reserve as a garnish.

Place the coral mixture in a bowl. Whisk 200 ml (7 fl oz) of sauce a little at a time on to the mixture. Stir into the sauce left in the pan. Heat, but do not allow to boil. Add chopped parsley.

Serve the conger steaks coated in sauce and garnished with pieces of lobster meat.

Note: It is possible to obtain 'crippled' lobsters from suppliers, at very reasonable rates. These are quite adequate. Conger balances well with a lobster sauce, not only because it has a good flavour, but also because its firm texture needs the long simmering.

Dodine de Pintade
Stuffed and Boned Guineafowl

Serves: 6. Total cost: 16 units. Preparation: 25–35 mins. Cooking: 1¼ hrs. Oven: 204°C/425°F/Gas Mk 7. Wine suggestion: Bordeaux – St. Estèphe.

Ingredients	
	1 guinea fowl about 1 kg (2¼ lb)
	450 g (1 lb) minced veal
	1 egg
	1 soupspoon cognac
	100 g (3½ oz) streaky bacon
	salt and pepper

Method: Bone the guinea fowl as for a galantine.

Mince the breast meat and add to the minced veal. Lightly beat the egg with the cognac. Mix into the farce. Season. Fill the leg cavities with the farce. Spread a layer of farce on the skin.

Season the leg meat. Arrange on the layer of farce. Cover the legs with the remaining farce.

Reconstitute the guinea fowl as nearly as possible to its original shape. Fasten loose skin with cocktail sticks. Place slices of streaky bacon over the guinea fowl. Place on a rack in a hottish oven. Roast for 1¼ hours.

Note: Use the bones and carcass to make a simple gravy. Brown bones and carcass in the oven. Place in a pan with one onion, one carrot, a soupspoon chopped celery leaves, bouquet garni and 1 litre of water.

Bring to the boil. Simmer uncovered for 2 hours. Skim regularly. Strain the sauce. Add a teaspoon of redcurrant jelly. Reduce to about 400 ml (14 fl oz). When the guinea fowl has cooked, take the pan underneath the rack to catch the juices. Remove any fat, use kitchen paper to soak it up. Add the stock to the juices. Dissolve 2 teaspoons of arrowroot in a soupspoon of cognac. Add to the gravy. Bring to the boil. Serve in a sauce boat.

Pain de Veau en Feuilletage

Veal Forcemeat in Puff Pastry

Serves: 8. Total cost: 14 units. Preparation: 20–30 mins. Cooking: 1¼ hrs. Other: the feuilletage. Oven: 15 mins at 215°C/420°F/Gas Mk 7, 45 mins at 180°C/356°F/Gas Mk 4. Wine suggestion: Bordeaux – St Julien.

Ingredients 500 g (18 oz) veal (any cheaper cut)
250 g (9 oz) lean pork
250 g (9 oz) fat pork
1 onion
50 g (scant 2 oz) butter
4 eggs
1 slice bread soaked in milk and squeezed out
1 soupspoon thyme
1 soupspoon parsley
salt and pepper
For the croûte:
1 kg (2¼ lb) feuilletage (see page 42)
1 egg yolk

Method: Cube the veal and the pork. Dice the onion. Sauté the meats, then the onion in the butter till they have coloured slightly. Cool. Blend together in the liquidiser.

Lightly beat the eggs and add to the meat. Continue blending. Work in the bread, the herbs and the seasoning.

Roll out a third of the pastry to form an oblong. Spread the veal mixture on this layer. Roll out the rest of the pastry. Cover the meat. Seal the edges with water. Place on an oiled piece of foil. Brush with egg yolk.

Place in a hot oven. After 15 minutes turn down the heat of the oven to moderate. Continue baking for a further 45 minutes.

Serve with a Hollandaise (page 40) or Béarnaise sauce.

243

Entrecôte Marchand de Vin
Entrecôte Steak with White Wine, Shallots and Butter

Serves: 8. Total cost: 31 units. Preparation: 20–25 mins. Cooking: 7–12 mins. Wine suggestion: Bordeaux – St Emilion.

Ingredients 8 × 200 g (7 oz) sirloin steaks
1 soupspoon meat glaze (page 24)
3 shallots
200 ml (7 fl oz) white wine
1 bayleaf
2 soupspoons parsley
140 g (5 oz) unsalted butter
pepper
(grilling oil, page 32)

Method: Dice the shallots. Place in a pan with wine and bayleaf. Boil. Reduce till only two soupspoons of liquid remain. Stir in the meat glaze. Beat in softened butter a few pieces at a time. Do not let the sauce boil. Stir in parsley. Pepper.

Brush the steaks with grilling oil. Grill as required. Spoon the sauce over each steak.

Note: This is not a sauce that can be made in advance and kept hot. However, if one has the wine/meat glaze base made, one may re-heat it and finish with the butter.

Sweets

Bûche de Noël
Christmas Yule Log

Serves: 8. Total cost: 5 units. Preparation: 35–45 mins. Cooking: 5 mins. Other: cooling génoise 1 hr. Oven: 235°C/455°F/Gas Mk 8.

Ingredients   *For the génoise:*
80 g (3 oz) castor sugar
80 g (3 oz) flour
30 g (1 oz) unsalted butter
3 large eggs
For the butter cream:
250 g (9 oz) granulated sugar
8 yolks
250 g (9 oz) unsalted butter
2 teaspoons good instant coffee
½ cube unsweetened baker's chocolate
For the meringue:
2 egg whites
100 g (3½ oz) castor sugar

Method: Make the génoise. Beat yolks and sugar to the ribbon. Stiffly beat whites. Melt butter. Fold flour into yolks/sugar mix. Fold in whites and melted butter. Line a baking tray with foil, so that it comes up the sides of the tray. Pour mixture over foil. Spread evenly, approximately 30 cm × 23 cm × 1½ cm (12 in × 9 in × ½ in). Place immediately in a hot oven. Bake 5 minutes. Cool.

Beat yolks (not straight out of the fridge). Boil sugar to soft ball (drop a little boiling sugar into cold water and it will form a soft ball). Whisk boiling sugar on to yolks. Continue whisking to cool the mixture (an electric mixer is a great help). Beat softened butter into the yolks mix. Melt chocolate and coffee with a tablespoon boiling water. Incorporate into the mixture. Fold in meringue.

Spread half the coffee/chocolate cream over the génoise. Roll up like a Swiss roll. Cut off a slice on the slant. Place on top of the roll to simulate a sawn-off branch. Pipe the rest of the cream over the bûche using a star tube. Finish the bark effect with a palette knife.

Note: Cake decoration is an avowed weakness of the author. However, one may, if not pressed for time, decorate the bûche with meringue mushrooms. Also one may decorate the ends with layered marzipan to give the impression of a sawn-off log.

Soufflé aux Mandarines
Mandarin Soufflé

Serves: 8. Total cost: 9 units. Preparation: 25–30 mins. Cooking: 10 mins. Oven: 235°C/455°F/Gas Mk 8.

Ingredients   8 mandarin oranges
200 g (7 oz) sugar lumps
30 g (1 oz) flour
30 g (1 oz) butter
5 eggs
(butter)

Method: Wash the mandarin skins thoroughly to remove chemicals. Rub the zests with sugar lumps.

Place the sugar in a pan. Stir in the juice of the mandarins. Make a roux with flour and butter. Add to the sugar. Take off the heat.

Separate the whites and yolks. Mix the yolks with the sugar, mandarins and flour. Beat the whites to stiff peaks. Fold into the mixture with a metal spoon.

Butter eight individual soufflé dishes. Chill in the freezer. Spoon the soufflé mix into the dishes. Smooth the tops. Using the tip of a knife free the mixture from the edges.

Bake in a very hot oven for about 10 minutes till the soufflé has risen.

Note: The difference between the soufflés made in a private home and a busy restaurant is that the time factor is all important. One cannot afford, generally speaking, to let the customer wait 25 minutes, the time it takes for a soufflé baked in a moderate oven to cook. Also, where portion control is relevant, individual soufflés make better sense.

Poires en Feuilletage
Pears in Puff Pastry

Serves: 8. Total cost: 6 units. Preparation: 20–30 mins. Cooking: 30 mins. Other: feuilletage. Oven: 220°C/428°F/Gas Mk 7.

247

Ingredients 8 pears
grated zest of a lemon
80 g (3 oz) soft brown sugar
2 teaspoons cinnamon
1 kg (2¼ lb) feuilletage (see page 42)
1 egg yolk

Method: Divide the pastry into eight equal parts. Roll out into pieces large enough to envelop the pears.

Peel the pears. Sift together the grated zest, sugar and cinnamon. Roll the pears in this mixture so they are well coated.

Wrap each pear in feuilletage. Seal the edges carefully with water. Brush with egg yolk. Bake in a hot oven for 30 minutes.

Serve either hot or cold.

Note: If one has a syringe available, one may inject a little pear alcohol or kirsch into each pear.

Serve with crème Chantilly to which a little pear alcohol (Poire Williams) has been added.

Gâteau aux Noix
Walnut Gâteau

Serves: 8. Total cost: 8 units. Preparation: 20–30 mins. Cooking: 40 mins. Other: rest after baking 24 hrs. Oven: in at 190°C/374°F/Gas Mk 5, down to 175°C/347°F/Gas Mk 4.

Ingredients 150 g (5½ oz) castor sugar
75 g (scant 3 oz) butter
75 g (scant 3 oz) flour
½ teaspoon baking powder
grated zest of a lemon
4 large eggs
150 g (5½ oz) ground walnuts
(butter and sugar for tin)

Garnish:
300 ml (10 fl oz) double cream
75 g (scant 3 oz) castor sugar
1 soupspoon kirsch
150 g (5½ oz) walnuts

Method: Beat the yolks of the eggs and the castor sugar together. When frothy beat in the melted butter. Incorporate the ground walnuts and the zest of lemon.

Sift the flour and baking powder. Stiffly beat the egg whites. Fold in alternately, a spoon at a time, egg white and flour.

Butter and sugar a cake tin. Pour the mixture into the tin. Place in a moderate oven. Turn down the temperature to warm. Bake 40 minutes. Turn out onto a cooling rack. Cool. Leave overnight.

Prepare the garnish. Whisk together the cream, sugar and kirsch till stiff. Divide the walnuts into two equal parts. Chop half of them and fold into half of the whipped cream. Slice the cake in half. Fill with the walnut cream. Spread the remainder of the cream on top of the gâteau. Decorate with the remaining walnuts.

Note: One leaves the gâteau overnight so that it is less indigestible.

Charlotte aux Marrons
Chestnut Charlotte

Serves: 8. Total cost: 9 units. Preparation: 45–60 mins. Cooking: biscuits 15 mins, chestnuts 40 mins. Other: to set the charlotte 8 hrs. Oven: 200°C/392°F/Gas Mk 6.

Ingredients	1 kg (2¼ lb) chestnuts	4 eggs
	1 jar (6 oz) stem ginger	115 g (4 oz) flour
	1 soupspoon cognac	vanilla essence
	150 g (5½ oz) butter	icing sugar
	1 litre (35 fl oz) milk	
	For the biscuits à la cuillère:	
	160 g (5½ oz) castor sugar	

Method: Prepare the biscuits à la cuillère. Beat the sugar and yolks to the ribbon. Add the vanilla essence. Stir in the flour. Beat the whites till stiff. Fold into the mixture. Fill a piping bag plus medium size plain tube with the mixture. Butter sheets of greaseproof paper on baking trays. Pipe 'fingers' of paste 4 cm (1½ in) apart on the trays (the mixture is right if it holds its shape without spreading). Dredge with icing sugar. Bake in a hot oven 15 minutes.

Blanch the chestnuts in boiling water 10 minutes. Peel the skins. Poach the chestnuts in milk until tender.

Blend chestnuts, stem ginger together with their syrup, butter and cognac in the liquidiser.

Line a charlotte mould with the biscuits à la cuillère. Fill the mould with the chestnut cream. Place in the fridge and leave at least 8 hours to set. Turn out the mould.

R

249

A Word About Customers

Customers are not units on a specialist consultant's graph. They have to be flattered, wooed and ultimately seduced one by one. Each satisfied member of the public is a conquest. As a result, the bistro owner is more a member of the school of Don Juan than of the Harvard School of Business Studies. Like Don Juan he shares a fundamental concern with other people's appetites. Like him he often has to overcome initial distrust and prejudice. His intentions, however, are pure, so hopefully the closest he comes to being engulfed in the inferno is when hovering over his ovens on a busy Saturday night.

Though he may be adept at handling projections, statistics and profit margins, the 'patron' knows that taste buds will be the final arbiters of whether the figures have any meaning or not. All very well but no two tastes, like sets of fingerprints, are alike.

It is impossible then to generalise the potential, satisfied customer or to tie him in with a social group based on age, affluence or education. Where one can draw a dividing line is between those who discriminate between the different things they eat and those who do not. The latter do not exclusively haunt the queues outside the fish and chip shop. They also eat at the Tour d'Argent in Paris and the Gavroche in London. Their ability to afford the most prestigious restaurants is no guarantee that they will enjoy their food.

A bistro depends for its revenue on entertaining those who discriminate and take an interest in what they eat. These are of two kinds, the bluff: 'I know what I like and that's what I want' brigade and the open minded. To know one's mind is not a weakness. Nor is it the same as narrow-mindedness. If this customer likes your crème brûlée he may patronise you once a week. If not, bad luck. Because the attitude is so common among those eating out, it is a brave proprietor who disregards it and serves only what pleases himself. At Chewton Glen Hotel (Egon Ronay's Hotel of the Year 1976) though the quality of the food and the capacity of the chef are both excellent, the menu retains its melon and its prawn cocktail, though it may cost a rosette or two.

The experience of those discriminating customers who retain open minds ranges from the accomplished epicure to the student taking out his first girlfriend. Of the former there cannot be more than a handful throughout the country. The latter group (not students specifically!) form the bottom of the pyramid, the potential market which the bistro owner hopes to attract; whether his clientèle is made up of regulars, passing trade, tourists, or holidaymakers is immaterial.

Unlike cigarettes, or the beer that refreshes the parts that other beers can't reach, restaurants cannot survive indefinitely on the strength of advertising campaigns. Their success depends on a reputation that they must fight tooth and nail to obtain.

Reputation comes, not via the inexperienced eaters returning home flushed after a good night out, nor though one might wish it so, from the expert criticism of a gourmet, unless he happens to write for one of the guides; it comes from the inexpert but experienced eaters who judge by comparing personal impressions of one meal with another.

These core customers make or break a place. Before peeling the first onion of the day one has to foresee the standards which they expect, standards relating to the food, though only indirectly. First they expect value for money. Criticism of the kind: 'Well, the food was all right, but the price, my dear – ridiculous,' will kill a restaurant stone dead unless it relies on overseas visitors. Second, one can lump together the niggling shortcomings that distract the attention from the food: lukewarm food, cold plates, hanging about between courses, wrongly taken orders, mistakes in the bills, 'soup's off' syndrome, the odd dirty dish or unpolished glass and high decibel quadrophonic music. These caveats apply to all customers whether they can tell the difference between butter and marge or not.

Having instanced the areas where one may antagonise a customer, regardless of the quality of the food, it is worth adding up the pluses that put a customer on one's side. Detailed and informed help with the menu must be one of the most neglected aspects of selling food. In order to do well, explanations must go beyond: 'It's lamb, sir, with a sort of sauce'. After all, one would expect more from the vacuum cleaner salesman than: 'It's for cleaning floors'. What applies to the food is equally important for the wine. It is a sorry day for gastronomy when the customer chooses his wine by the shape of the bottle.

Many years ago the author was refused a second pat of butter for his bread in an Auchterarder hotel on the grounds that it was against company policy. Whatever the additional cost, care over fresh bread, adequate butter, iced water, flowers if possible, all tip the scales in favour of a restaurant. Ironically, the offenders who serve plastic rolls are often giving away profits in peanuts, pearl onions and gherkins.

Sooner or later one faces the relevance of atmosphere and décor. A meal in pleasant surroundings enhances the food. 'Pleasant surroundings' mean different things to the French and the English which challenge the whole notion of 'bistro style'. Bistros in England do their business in the evenings. Dependent on their type they have candles in bottles and strings of garlic or a subtle lighting effect efficiently programmed by the interior designer. Each alternative builds on the assumption that one is furnishing romantic, escapist entertainment. This is really phoney romanticism.

The word 'bistro' itself is used as argot for a café. It need not automatically be an eating place. But let us adopt the extended meaning. When a French couple eats out (for convenience sake assume them to be the counterpart of the 'inexpert but experienced' group) they too expect entertainment. What would immediately strike them as incongruous would be candlelight or any form of subdued lighting. The lady's eyes might sparkle brighter, but the colours of the food are harder to discern and picking out the brownish tints of old Burgundy is well-nigh impossible. As for music, a Tzigane orchestra might be an amusing curiosity, but it would be a distraction from the main sources of entertainment, the food – and each other's company.

Cramped space, inelegant cutlery and paper napkins, the French couple will accept these if the dinner is excellent. So, one hopes, will the English counterpart. As the food sinks into the upper stomach and the fume of wine in moderation rises to the brain, the sense of well-being transcends any lack of surface comfort.

Atmosphere generates naturally as soon as one's premises are filled by people eating with relish. It's not the singing band of waiters in sailor suits who create the tone.

There is a false impression that because the French take eating seriously one ought to show reverence to every morsel that passes through one's lips and fervent approval for the first sip of the most modest wine. Truth is that 'great' meals like great wines are rare, even if one is fortunate enough to be able to eat in world-famous restaurants. For a meal to become great the party eating together must co-operate to the full with the food and wine. Because latent in most of us is the desire to applaud, there is always a temptation to throw away superlatives. To counter ape-like approval which claps to order by a conscious reserve is the mark of the truly discriminating customer. He is learning every time he eats; the chef learns every day he steps into the kitchen. Give him quality, and pleasure and relaxation beam through his mask.

Picture the pastiche Michelin man hunched in the corner of the restaurant, making mental notes about the fifth Sole Bonne Femme he has eaten in a month. Behind his oyster eyes he carries the memory of a thousand bad meals. But he, too, has had his godlike moments when the careful reticence has shattered, giving way before a Chartreuse de Brochet aux Epinards.

Most customers know the feeling when the owner or his representative approaches the table: 'Did you enjoy your meal?' 'Yes, very nice.' And the incident passes off with the minimum of fuss. This dialogue is usually the only human, if one may call it that, contact passing between client and 'bistro' symbolised by whoever pops the question. The opportunity for either side to sound the other fades. Why was the sauce thin, what seasoning in the terrine, how to stuff the breast of chicken, the unusual texture of the pastry. All the quirks and curiosity which might cross an interested customer's mind are unasked and unanswered. True, few people can take more than a minute's lecturing on a full stomach and the attention of the 'patron' to the customer's welfare may seem an intrusion of privacy. But the customer, unaware of it though he may be, is the most potent member of a bistro's sales force. His recommendation is listened to because he receives no commission on it. The more he is primed, the better he will sell.

A select band of food writers tour the country transforming their impressions of restaurants into print. Their opinions carry the weight of the printed word. They bless with the gift of free publicity. They provide the cuttings that one tucks away in the files, but it is the reputation one has earned from the paying public that keeps one afloat. The analogy with the theatre is at once striking. A bistro performs and entertains in much the same way. More than a play or revue, it invites its customers to return time and again with the expectation of finding something new each time.

Index

255